ABOUT THE AUTHOR

Because of her authorship of this book, the first study of the dog-man relationship by a dog, Dido was invited by the Kennel Club to appear in the 1992 Parade of Dog Personalities at Cruft's. She also received a letter of congratulation and thanks from HM the Queen for sending her a copy signed with her now famous paw-mark. Dido is the first canine author to be listed in the Authors' Catalogues of great libraries and the first to open her own bank account for her royalties. Now four years old, Dido has become Britain's most famous dog, with many appearances on television, radio and at lectures and other public events which have done much to popularize the little-known chocolate strain of the Labrador breed.

ABOUT HER CHAP

Dido's literary 'ghost', Chapman Pincher, is best known for his writings about espionage but, after establishing close communication with Dido, he decided to use his investigative skills in the cleaner world of dogs, where treachery and 'disinformation' are unknown. Trained as a zoologist, he was able to put himself inside Dido's skin, and, by thinking like a dog, to experience the world as she does. This enabled Dido to explain why the dog-human relationship is so uniquely close. To his surprise, he also found himself recording Dido's candid views on people, especially himself.

A countryman, he and Dido live in the village of Kintbury in Berkshire, spending much time together fishing on the River Kennet and, inseparably, in his study, answerin̶̶̶̶̶̶̶̶̶̶̶̶̶̶̶̶̶̶ her next book.

D0594820

ONE DOG
AND HER MAN

by Dido

assisted by
CHAPMAN PINCHER

BANTAM BOOKS
LONDON · NEW YORK · TORONTO · SYDNEY · AUCKLAND

To the Greater Glory of Dog

ONE DOG AND HER MAN
A BANTAM BOOK 0 553 40439 3

Originally published in Great Britain by
George Weidenfeld & Nicolson Ltd.

PRINTING HISTORY
George Weidenfeld edition published 1991
Bantam edition published 1992
Bantam edition reprinted 1993

Set in 10pt Linotype Palatino by
Chippendale Type Ltd., Otley, West Yorkshire.

Bantam Books are published by Transworld Publishers Ltd.,
61–63 Uxbridge Road, Ealing, London W5 5SA,
in Australia by Transworld Publishers (Australia) Pty. Ltd.,
15–25 Helles Avenue, Moorebank, NSW 2170,
and in New Zealand by Transworld Publishers (N.Z.) Ltd.,
3 William Pickering Drive, Albany, Auckland.

Printed and bound in Great Britain by
Cox & Wyman Ltd., Reading, Berks.

CONTENTS

Foreword by Chapman Pincher

I'll make a ghost of him that lets me

It is commonly said that a day without wine is a day without sunshine. I feel the same way about dogs. People and dogs have shared the same circumstances in a uniquely intimate relationship for many centuries. No animal more closely resembles man in temperament. As both are pack animals by inherited nature, their emotional needs are similar, which is why the relationship was possible and became so successful. Like us they crave regular companionship, contact and affection. If one of the deepest requirements of human nature is to be wanted and appreciated so it is of canine nature.

Scientists therefore believe that the study of canine behaviour can tell us a great deal about our own — what makes some people loners and others gregarious, some aggressive, others timid, some endearing, others unlikeable, some lazy, others energetic and so on. My own observations would endorse that concept, especially in the case of Dido, my ninth dog and first Labrador, who epitomizes the spirit of dogliness more than any other I have encountered.

By making a sustained effort to put myself inside Dido's skin, with a dog's eye view of the world and thinking like a dog, I have learned a great deal, becoming much more understanding of her behaviour and more aware of my previous inadequacies in the man-dog relationship.

Through the close bond we have established in the process, she has heightened my perception of canine capabilities and I am grateful to her for making me appreciate her point of view on many matters. She has also taught me quite a lot about myself, as her somewhat satirical, tongue-in-jowl musings, communicated so frankly in this book, clearly demonstrate. Honesty and openness are probably the soundest basis for any relationship requiring mutual understanding and if you cannot be entirely honest with another human being – as few can – at least you can be with your dog. So I take her feelings in the spirit in which they are expressed.

Some years ago, the behavioural scientist Elizabeth Borgese, daughter of Thomas Mann, the German novelist, trained a dog to type on a specially built typewriter with keys two inches in diameter. Using its nose, the dog learned to type, from dictation, whole words like bad, sad, dog, good, ball, dear and fear. However, agile as she is, Dido could not possibly use my word processor so I have been privileged to act as her literary secretary – an adoguensis – and transcribe the many canine concepts which, I believe, she has managed to communicate to me through her several channels and transfer into my skull. Like many other dogs, Dido is quite eloquent to those prepared to pay close attention and to try to understand.

In my sojourns inside her skin other concepts and views which I imagine she would like to convey on behalf of her kind came to mind so I have also articulated into English what I fancy Dido would like to put on record, had she the means of doing so.

She fulfils the dictionary definition of 'author' in that she is the originator of the book, and the function of a

8

'ghost', in which capacity I have served her, is to write what the author would state if she had the capability. Any 'ghost' is generally given licence to interpret the views and describe the experiences of the individual whose name appears on the title page, and if I have too freely mistranslated, misinterpreted or exaggerated what I believe Dido has conveyed to me, or would like to, I am entirely to blame.

As is customary with ghosted books, and especially autobiographies, the text is presented in the first person as though entirely written by the author. In this respect, apart from being a dog, Dido does not differ from several famous people of my acquaintance.

No doubt, pedants will object to the approach as being altogether too anthropomorphic, with human attributes being assigned to a dog on an unacceptable scale by a 'ghost' smitten with caninomania, but this is not a book for pedants, whether scientists, breeders or trainers. It is for dog lovers who massively out-number them. I am confident that Dido would regard the criticism as of small consequence so long as she gets her messages across to a wide audience in a readable manner, and as being more than balanced by the caninomorphic interpretations.

I apologize in advance for the fractured quotations, which could literally be described as doggerel, and for the occasional puns which the author seems unable to resist.

It may seem incredible that Dido should have authored a book but, in my eyes, she happens to be a remarkable dog, as I expect your dog is in yours. I have been blessed with wonderful dogs in my long life but Dido is so magical that anything seems possible. She certainly has a mind of her own, great determination and more than her fair share of feminine wiles. Anyway, everybody else in the house has produced a book so why shouldn't Dido? 'Dog writes Book' should be an even better headline than 'Man bites Dog'.

Perhaps she will become a best-selling dog meriting VID treatment which, I fear, she already gets from me as reward for enriching my life and providing so many keys to the kingdom of dog.

We have discussed with our local bank manager the various legal aspects of Dido's possible finances. He was most sympathetic and, with the butcher just a few yards up the road, advised a joint account, pointing out that, provided there was mutual trust between us, which, of course, there is, trustees would be unnecessary. On those terms he concluded, 'I shall be delighted to include Dido as a customer of the Bank and await your further instructions.'

We may also have some difficulty in convincing the taxman that she authored the book but, win or lose, that encounter will also be unique.

So let us give Dido her head and see what we get. She knows that I am bound to forgive her for any liberties, however outrageous.

Chapman Pincher
Kintbury, Berks.
1991

Introduction: Dog's Best Friend

Oh wad some Pow'r the giftie gie ye
To see yoursels as doggies see ye!
It wad frae mony a blunder free ye,
And foolish notion.

Hundreds of books have been written about dogs by people. Invariably they refer to us as 'man's best friend' with lots of advice on how we should be treated to get the best from the man-dog relationship. The time has come for a serious book about 'dog's best friend' and how he should be treated to get the best out of the dog-man relationship. Only a dog could produce it.

Much has also been recorded about the effects of human culture on us. What about the effects of canine culture on you? We influence the lives of countless millions of you in many ways, if you think about it – in home life, work and sport. Many of you who are blind, deaf or otherwise disabled are dependent on us. Over the centuries poems, songs and books have been written in praise of us and we appear in many famous paintings. We are renowned in your mythology. Flowers, a fish and a star are named after us. So are air combats and even a guided missile.

My Chap, as I prefer to call my master, used to be a zoologist when he was young, and had been contemplating a book about dog behaviour using his investigative skills and the results of new scientific research. I have beaten him to it with a book about the canine predicament as experienced through the eyes, nose and brain of a dog and in the light of my own instincts, knowledge and research. In the process, which has taken me hundreds of dog-hours, I propose to reveal how we really feel about human behaviour, which we often witness in a uniquely private way when you think you are alone. I also hope to straighten out some misconceptions on both sides and so make the dog-man alliance more realistic. My Chap has lots of books about dogs in his study and is more understanding than most about a dog's true nature. This has made it much easier for me to communicate my thoughts to him but he still has much to learn, both about me and the ordinary dog in the street. There is still mystery about us dogs – especially the females of the species!

I also intend to strike a few blows for dogkind, of which the proper study is dog. Though we don't deserve to be, we are at your mercy but we have our rights, deriving not just from the fact that we exist but from the exceptional contribution we have made to human civilization. I am well qualified for the task of expounding them as I also am for pointing out the oddities of the human species. It is surprising what we witness when people have let their guard down and regard themselves as being quite alone. The secret self is a peculiarly human feature and we dogs see you as you really are because you don't try to hide anything from us as you do from everybody else, even those you love and, perhaps, especially from those you love. Many men, in particular, are inhibited in displaying their emotions to another human being but not to a dog. It is not that they don't want to show their love or sorrow to another person but find it difficult and even unmanly to do so, while they have no such problem with a dog. I suspect that I get a lot of affection and praise that should be lavished on the Chap's wife for what she does for us all. Many men seem prepared to 'spoil' a dog but not a wife.

I'll make no bones about it, my Chap is as odd a human being as any, as my narrative will reveal. He is a work fanatic because he can't stop and is so governed by time that he won't waste a minute. He does little for the sheer sake or pleasure of it, which is the only reason I do anything at all. Everything he does must always have a further purpose.

He cannot bear to throw away a scrap of paper until nothing more can be written on it. As a result he has mounds of it which he will never live long enough to use. In fact he is a slave to paper, like so many other men, and I have often heard him say that he will be found dead under a heap of it. Nevertheless he goes on collecting it. I might collect a few bones but not to that ludicrous extent.

Time and again, I have heard him declare that he will never spend another penny on the garden when some insect, mould or I, myself, ruin one of his plants yet he remains unable to pass the garden centre and I watch him stagger out with new extravagances. He repeatedly deludes himself into making excuses into reasons. Like every other human whom I have encountered he affects to have principles yet he trims them when it suits.

He rages at his word processor when he is summoned by bleeps and thinks it has gone wrong – 'Oh shut up! I'm coming' – and I have heard him threaten to stove it in if it repeats an error. Oddly, the threat seems to work but if I flew off the handle like that he would think I was going mad. I have even heard him apologize to the machine when it has cried out in pain and he has belatedly found that some fault was his own – as he has often apologized to me for similar reasons. It is the same with the terrible things he calls other drivers though he knows they can't

13

hear him. Still, I suppose that every man is entitled to his bark, especially when, as in the Chap's case, it is so much worse than his bite.

Time and again I hear his wife call, 'What was that? I can't hear you.' Answer – 'Oh nothing. I was just talking to Dido.' He even talks to George, the canary who lives in the conservatory, and to Bobby, the tame robin in the garden. I could many another tale unfold, as most dogs could.

I have no wish to appear manmatic but, while I am driven to admit to the superiority of human intelligence, so far as cleverness is concerned, dogs are, in many respects, wiser; wisdom in my book being the ability to make sensible use of your knowledge. Human beings pride themselves on their intelligence but, to my simple mind, their sanity, as judged by their behaviour, is largely a mask. So many people are really so different from the persona they present, as we dogs notice while we watch and listen quietly. There is the mask made necessary by the demands of sociability, when the face you have to show may be very different from the face your real feelings would reveal. There is the mask that hides your secret thoughts, the most impenetrable of all. We do not live behind any mask, which is what 'persona' originally meant. The 'canina' I present is me as I really am and I think that is more honest.

Even your physical appearance is artificial and dependent on clothes, cosmetics, jewellery and hair-dyes, of which we have no need. Though artists rave about the beauty of the nude human form, the rest of you seem to be ashamed of it and keep parts of it covered at all costs. All I have to do to look and feel beautiful is to sit in a patch of sunshine, as nature made me. Or even to roll on my back for, having no cause for shame, we dogs have no private parts.

Have you ever stopped to think how much of your life is spent in fantasy – in day-dreams and reading and

14

watching fiction? You spend so much of your life trying to identify with others, whom you would rather be, instead of being yourself. The word 'romantic', which women in particular use with such yearning, most of the time means 'remote from ordinary life'. We dogs are down-to-earth realists and have to be. There are no Walter Mittys in the dog world. Yours is full of them.

So here goes! I do not know what my enterprise will do for my relationship with the Chap, especially if I out-sell him on the bookstalls, but it is a risk I will have to take. I suppose that I am already taking a risk in having my name on this book when I am incapable of checking the proofs to see what I am alleged to have contributed to this joint experiment at being a mouthpiece for dogkind. There is little I can do if my 'ghost' has exceeded his brief and gone over the top. Can a dog sue for false representation? Or even for libel? An interesting prospect when damages are so great these days. An owner can certainly sue on behalf of a dog if, for example, somebody wrote that a valuable stud dog was infertile or carried some bad genes. But I suppose that I shall just have to put my trust in human integrity. That's dog's eternal lot.

1 About Me

Oh what a piece of work is a dog

On my pedigree certificate I am called Keneven Fantasy but I answer to Dido and you may think that is a funny name, as a lot of people do when my Chap calls it across the Common, though shouting 'Keneven Fantasy!' would be even funnier. But Dido was the name of a famous and beautiful Princess who founded the ancient city of Carthage in Africa. Nobody really knows what she looked like but perhaps she was chocolate coloured like I am – all over, even my nose. She must have been beautiful for even Shakespeare mentions her – 'In such a night stood Dido . . .' The Chap, who fancies himself as a know-all, only remembers one thing about her from his schoolboy days of studying Virgil's long poem *The Aeneid* – that she used to lie on a 'lofty couch'. That has not done me much good because whenever I try to emulate her I get turfed off. Still, I like being called Dido and now that Fido, which just meant faithful, is out of fashion I am not likely to be confused with anyone else. (Nobody I know has ever encountered a dog called Fido, though I have met a man with that name.) Perhaps someone will write a poem about me one day. Just a short one. I think I would like to be the dark bitch of somebody's sonnet. A pity the Chap isn't a poet.

17

I am a three-year-old Labrador, so-called because my breed was created in Newfoundland, an island off the coast of Labrador, in Canada. Why Labrador was given that name seems to be in doubt but the Chap has a theory that the country was called after the dog because *labros* is Greek for 'greedy' and Labrus was, therefore, a common name for a dog in ancient Rome – one of his endless jokes about me, of course.

In reality, according to an authoritative book in my Chap's library, we were bred by the commercial fishermen to retrieve cod and other fish which happened to escape from the hooks on the long-lines when almost landed. Those dogs also assisted netting operations by swimming between boats and the shore with ropes and even the corners of nets in their mouths. Others were used to extract salmon out of shallow rivers, as wolves and bears still do. So there are good reasons why we Labradors are such strong swimmers, love water and do not feel the cold even in a rough winter sea. I suppose we could be called sea-dogs. The Chap's wife even thinks I might be partly descended from a seal because I can splay my back legs flat on the ground and bounce forwards on my belly by nodding my head up and down.

The fish connection may also explain why we are so intelligent. There is a growing belief that fish flesh contains the special raw materials needed for brain growth in other creatures as well as humans. No doubt the fishermen fed their pups on fish rather than meat because it would be cheaper and more easily available. Hence the remarkable Labrador brain.

My ancestors were imported to Britain by traders in salt cod in the middle years of the nineteenth century. They were immigrants, coloured immigrants in fact, but they were warmly welcomed by the gentry because they were as good at retrieving game birds as retrieving fish. Now we are an established part of

18

the British country scene, including the Royal scene. Labradors, as we became known in Britain, have enjoyed the Royal patronage for many years. The corgis get the media attention but, from what I have heard, the Queen derives her greatest joy from working her Labrador gun dogs at pheasant and grouse shoots, operating well back behind the shooting line for the most difficult birds. It has been said that a cat can look at the Queen. Dogs do it all the time.

Most Labradors are black or yellow but a select few of us are chocolate and that is the proper name for my colour, used by the breeders and those who show dogs at places like Crufts. Chocolate Labradors are popular for showing but I am not destined to be a show-dog. I would rather win the Booker Prize than be Supreme Champion at Crufts.

I am the colour of bitter chocolate, though there is nothing bitter about me. I am a very happy dog – I cannot say 'gay dog' safely these days – with a capacity to spread happiness around me. Happiness is dog-shaped, I say. In fact if I hadn't been called Dido I would like to have been called Happy.

The only things black about me are my whiskers, my claws and the pupils of my eyes and the only thing yellow about me is my collar, a big, wide one bought at Harrods in London and with my telephone number on it. I used to have a brown collar but after my Chap and his wife had tripped over me a few times in the half-darkness, which camouflages me too well, they decided that they needed to be able to see me more clearly in all our interests.

Like all dogs, we Labradors are directly descended from wolves, which still live in Northern Canada. This has been proved to the satisfaction of scientists from examination of skulls, blood factors and chromosomes – the strings of genes, of which I and the wolf each have 78 compared with your 46. So, deep inside, in my habits, racial memories and reflexes, I am still to a considerable extent a wolf in dog's clothing. In spite of their evil reputation in fairy tales, wolves are splendid animals. They have also been on the earth for something like 20 million years. So the first thing I would like to establish is that, as wolves, we were here long before you. Also, whatever most humans think about them, I'd rather be descended from a wolf than from an ape. While you may have accepted your descent from creatures like apes you do not seem to be proud of it. I am proud to be descended from the wolf.

It is from our wolf ancestors that we inherited the special features that have made our close alliance with you possible. By nature the dog and the human are both pack animals, submitting to a leader, and from that common feature everything else has flowed. I regard my Chap as the pack leader, which is why, when I have to be, I am deferential to him and show him fidelity, though I can take more liberties with him than I would dare with the canine leader of a pack. There is no harm in letting my Chap think he is in command but an astute female gets her way in the end. Usually when I roll over in the submissive posture I would present to the canine pack leader I simply want my belly scratched. I say *my* Chap for, to my way of reckoning, I own him as much as he owns me, as part of the pack.

Being pack animals by nature we can feel very insecure when we are alone. In the wild it was dangerous to be alone, as it was for your ancestors. That is the primeval reason why we so much prefer to live in the house with the human pack rather than be banished to a kennel outside. While the creature comforts are much appreciated they are secondary. The myth that dogs are healthier if kept outside was probably concocted by excessively house-proud women and others have come to believe it or latched on to it.

The lone wolf was the odd wolf out and his eerie howl was a cry of loneliness. To this day, a rogue wolf expelled from its pack howls its agony to the moon but such an unhappy creature rarely lasts long. Perhaps it finds its life not worth living, as many people do when deprived of human contact. So, while there may be some dogs who are natural loners the great majority of us, including me, detest loneliness and find it very hard to bear. It is truly terrible for a gregarious dog to be shut up all alone. It can have a wonderful kennel and run but on its own it suffers. Is there anything more heart-rending than the repeated howl of the lonely dog, unless it be the quiet tears of human loneliness?

Like humans we each have a threshold for loneliness before it begins to bite and mine is very low. I begin to feel lonely in a few minutes, which is why I would always rather be taken in the car even if I am not allowed out of it. Sometimes at night I find the odd shoe belonging to the Chap or his wife and have it in bed with me. Or I might borrow an item of washing off the clotheshorse and have even been reduced to the dishcloth. Whatever it is, it helps to remind me that I am not really alone and, come the morning, I shall be back in the bosom of the pack. If I ever felt utterly lonely then I might express it with a high-pitched rendering of 'Dido's Lament'.

Our inborn fear and hatred of loneliness is the reason why we give you such a warm welcome when you come home – we are not only delighted to see you but greatly relieved. Like you, we give companionship because we have such a deep-rooted need for it ourselves. By its inherited nature, no dog is an island entire of itself.

We were domesticated about 10,000 years ago, which was about the period when people began to live in encampments or villages so we have been intimate members of human society for so long that we are, unquestionably, the oldest domesticated animal. The horse and goat are not far behind but their size and habits hardly fitted them to be house companions. They also suffered from another disadvantage. They could not thrive on the same food as humans. We could and that coincidence must have been a major factor in establishing the man-dog relationship.

At that time, when man was a hunter, his way of life was close to that of a wolf and our ancestors probably frequented his encampments scavenging for scraps. As they would have been useful for giving early warning at night about the approach of marauders, animal or human, they may have been gradually encouraged to hang around. Then, perhaps, the women found puppies and tamed them for it has been shown that it is easy to hand-rear wolf cubs. They could then be used for tracking and hunting but probably even more for companionship, at which we excel to such a degree that recent research has shown that dog owners tend to be substantially healthier, physically and mentally, than the dogless. Tests have shown that stroking a dog lowers the human blood pressure. I don't know what it does to mine but I love it.

Our tendency to bark at strangers, animal or human, remains with us, for reasons I will explain later, and is very useful when so many criminals and vandals are about. A dog you know may be better than a dog you don't know but, these days, a man your dog knows (and approves of) is better than a man it doesn't know.

Perhaps Stone Age Dog adopted man, rather than the other way round, by hanging around his dwellings, keeping the area clean by scavenging his rubbish and showing what nice and useful creatures we are at heart. So I like to think that we dogesticated man.

Whichever way round it was we could truly be said to have 'gone to the men'. Both had to be willing partners to the alliance but it was much harder on our part.

We had to overcome the need to escape from man, the most ruthless, efficient and indiscriminate killer of all time. Yet we did it. Because we were used to trusting our own pack it was possible to trust man. Once forged, the bond offered such advantages to both partners that it became indissoluble and will, I believe, always remain so. My Chap and I share the belief that those who do not experience the dog-man relationship miss one of the most rewarding joys life has to offer.

I don't know why man came to call us 'dogs', which is Anglo-Saxon. But it probably does mean that it was one of the early words he invented because it is so short. If you think about it, early man would have used short words for the most important things in his life, 'man' being one of them. In most other languages the word for dog is short.

I am what my Chap calls 'a properly proportioned' dog – with the same shape as my wolf ancestors. That was the result of thousands of years of natural selection to produce the best machine for the environment and the tough conditions it imposed. Since man got hold of us he has changed us by the process called selection into more than 150 different breeds, worldwide. He has been able to do this quickly because of our short lifespan. We live only about one seventh as long as you so, since man got control of us, we have gone through about 4,000 generations, while man has gone through only 400. His strange 'fancies', the result of what is called 'cosmetic breeding', have led to the production of some breeds which, nice though they are, are certainly not proportioned as Nature intended. In fact, though I do not want to be unkind, some of them are freaks. For instance, the basset hound and dachshund which have ludicrously short legs, are the canine counterparts of those large-headed human circus dwarfs, who are also very good-natured and

23

companionable but would much rather not be that shape. My eyes, unlike those of the Pekingese and the King Charles spaniel, are not so peculiarly shaped and positioned that I get trouble with my tear ducts. My ears do not get into my bowl when I eat, as a spaniel's do. My chest does not compress my respiratory system and cause breathing difficulties, as it does in the bulldog. My skin is not too big for my body, as it is in the bloodhound. It is loose enough but not so loose that it gets into enormous folds that cause irritation.

I am neither a dwarf nor a giant, being what is described as of 'normal' canine height – 21 inches at the shoulder. The giant breeds, like the Great Dane and wolfhound, tend to have a short life span while the miniature breeds are the result of the continued selection of the runts in litters – the opposite of natural selection, which favours the strongest. The trend for extreme miniaturization must be deleterious because the smaller the brain the less its capability. There is, however, one advantage in being small – the higher the proportion of brain size to body weight, the longer the average life of the breed. Thus in mastiffs, which are old at seven, the body is so big that the proportion is about 1 to 340. In pekes, which often live to sixteen and beyond, it is about 1 to 95.

My chest is large and deep, housing a big heart and lungs, my waist trim and my legs are not bandy or knock-kneed. They are built for running down fast prey. Like your early ancestors, we relied on animals much bigger than ourselves for food and had to hunt them in packs which harried them to exhaustion, many paws and many jaws making it lighter work. So when I go I can really move, loping along on tiptoe and tipfinger for many miles, if necessary.

Like most of you, I am right-handed, preferring to use my front right paw when reaching for something, when 'pointing' at possible prey or trying to catch someone's attention, though I am not an habitual paw-giver. As with humans, one side of the dog brain is dominant over the other. This makes some dogs right-handed and some left-handed though few people ever notice it. (Frankly, I had not really noticed it myself until the Chap spotted it. He watches my behaviour so minutely that it is sometimes disconcerting. It's the Old Zoologist coming out. Still, it's better than being ignored and it keeps him occupied.)

There is nothing 'shaggy' about me. My coat is short but dense and glossy, with a soft undercoat, which I moult in the spring, and an overcoat of longer hairs, which I moult in the autumn. It is so water-repellent that it could be raining men and women and it wouldn't bother me. I keep warm in the coldest weather and such is my blood circulation that I can stand in freezing snow and my paws will not feel cold. Other naturally beautiful creatures, like the leopard and ocelot, have been hunted to near-extinction to give women spotty coats. My coat is so admired that, had there been a fashion for dog fur, I might not be alive to write this now.

I never have need for any artificial coat of the kind imposed by some owners on their dogs. Again, I don't wish to be rude about any of my fellow country-dogs but 'the apparel oft proclaims the dog'. Further, I am not so heavily clothed that I am troubled by heat and need trimming. In those lovely summers of 1989 and 1990 I was able to lie in the full sun and really enjoy it. Incidentally, it is not true that we dogs cannot sweat to keep cool except from our tongues and pads. We do have some sweat glands dotted over our skin but, as they are covered with hair, evaporation does not help much so they are not as efficient as yours, which are all over your body.

My muzzle is broad, not snipey, like some Labradors. My skull is wide to accommodate a large brain. My almond-shaped eyes are dark amber and properly set

25

in their sockets with no danger of popping out, as those of some pekes often do. They are set at a slight angle on my head to give me a wide range of vision so it is very difficult to creep up on me unobserved.

Because smell is easily my main sense I need a big nose set well in front of the rest of my body so that it is the first thing to confront any situation. In the past I also needed large jaws to hunt and kill large prey. With you, eyesight is your main sense so you need eyes facing plumb in front to give you binocular vision. You do not need such a big nose or large jaws so you have a flat face. Otherwise, our faces are basically the same. Indeed, my Chap says that there are days when everybody looks like dogs.

I have all my teeth – 42 of them, 20 upper and 22 lower, compared with 32 for you, if you have managed to hang on to them all, which seems to be rare, in spite of all your tooth-brushing and visits to the dentist. (I see that someone has marketed canine toothpaste made, as one might have guessed, in Hollywood but it has not been inflicted on me yet.)

Unlike so many dogs, I also have all my tail, a nice fat tail like an otter's, which is fitting for such a water-lover. The Chap says otters are delightful though when he was younger he used to hunt them, another human contradiction! My tail helps me to balance when I run and, as I will explain later, it is an important organ of communication. On my front paws, I even have my dewclaws, the remnants of my thumbs, which are so often removed from puppies by vets. I am very glad to have them because I have become adept at using them like thumbs for grasping a bone or someone's hand if I want him to go on tickling me. I can exert a much tighter grip than a dog with no dewclaws. Together with the little protruding pads above them, they make my paws more like hands and we wouldn't have them if they were of no use. They enable me to lie on my back and juggle with a large ball which, I suppose, is my party piece, causing much merriment when I am in the mood for it.

I weigh 65 pounds and I am very strong for my size. My Chap says that the muscle of 'beasts', which include me, is more powerful than human muscle, pound for pound, and it can release its energy more explosively. You will find that we are even more formidable if you tangle with us down at our level. When anyone tries to grab me my reactions are swifter than those of any human boxer, who would never be beaten if he could sway away from a punch as quickly and with as little effort as I can.

I leave it to others to say whether I am beautiful or not. Actually they never stop saying it. Everybody says I am beautiful – people even stop the Chap in the street to say so. One formidable lady who was in a group of dog experts – I believe that they call themselves cynologists – paid me the compliment of saying that I was 'beautifully put together'. Professional photographers agree and say that I am very photogenic, especially in colour. People also say that I have charm, which is something that can get both dog and man out of all sorts of difficulties. I have even heard someone remark that I have 'charisma'. I know that in stating all this I am revealing my streak of vanity but I think that it is minuscule compared with the usual human allotment.

It is said that people come to look like their dogs so if my Chap and his wife come to look like me they shouldn't do too badly.

Just as people have different personalities so we have different caninities and, according to scientists, they fall into four basic types – lively and active, irascible and wild, calm and imperturbable, dull and passive. I have no doubt which I belong to – the first, lively and active, and my Chap agrees. My caninity is extrovert.

27

I am an action dog, high on sociability and generous with affection. The capacity to form deep personal attachments to others is rated highly by psychologists who study human personality and I certainly have that. I am even-tempered, never ill-disposed. I am never miserable, as some dogs are to an extent which has led to the phrase 'hang-dog look'. Whatever I do I do it with enthusiasm and the joy of living.

Temperament is an important component of caninity and varies between breeds and within breeds. The dog-man relationship usually works well only if dog and owner are of similar temperament.

Like most of my breed, I am a smiler, a pleasure-giving characteristic which is also said to be inherited, and I reckon that I have a good sense of humour, a capacity for fun which is a sign of a mature personality in the human. So much so that my Chap says, 'She's a laugh a minute.' I find it fun, for instance, to shake myself all over the Chap when I have been in the water. After the third time it stretches *his* sense of humour though he does appreciate the way a wet shake, involving muscles you hardly possess, gets rid of water for which humans need a towel. Life should be mainly about fun shouldn't it? Dogs that can make people laugh can write their own tickets, as the saying is, and there is nothing like causing a laugh for banishing anger at something a dog has done. Does man get more fun out of the dog than the dog does out of man? It is a moot point. Speaking personally, or rather caninely, I think that man is the more laughable.

Curiously, smiling seems to be something we have copied from you because wolves do not smile in the wild, though they learn to do so in captivity. Considering the way wolves have been reviled and treated by humans they have not had much to smile about have they? In the few parts of the world where they still exist they continue to be shot on sight.

Whatever I may think about myself it's what my Chap thinks I am that's important in my life. He doesn't like a cowed dog and I am certainly not that. What is needed in a house-dog is a nice balance between timidity and overconfidence. I am not aggressive but I have plenty of spirit and am not afraid to show it when I am in the mood. Nobody can deny that I have style. I walk with confidence and don't slink along, as some dogs do. Admittedly, I do not have humility, which is supposed to be a good thing, but very few of you do, either. I am, in fact, rather adept at drawing attention to myself. But then, a lot of men and women I have met are good at that, too.

I regard myself as a thoroughly modern, emancipated dog but not so stupid as to be an ardent feminist. Above all, I am very much an individual. As my Chap puts it, 'Whatever she is she is the only one of it'. I like that.

2 How I Got My Chap

In mastery there is bondage:
In bondage there is mastery.

When I was born in the county of Devonshire, one of seven puppies, the time came, as it always must, for me to be found a home. Because I was well-bred – my grandfather was a Crufts champion, though of course I never met him or my father – I was sold for quite a high price to a young lady who spent most of her time with horses. She lived alone and was very kind. It was she who called me Dido.

It is very important that when we are pups we should be handled and petted a lot, especially between the third and fourteenth weeks, to establish the bond with humans and, fortunately, I had been. It is during that period that we become social creatures and 'imprinted' on the rest of the pack, as scientists put it. In the wild we would be fondled by the rest of the canine pack. If we are regularly handled by humans at that time we can also become imprinted on them and recognize them, probably by their odour, as members of our pack. Good breeders, as mine were, will fondle their pups a lot during those crucial weeks. If a pup fails to experience any contact with human beings before it is fourteen weeks old it can never become completely socialized and may remain withdrawn and even unapproachable.

A pup taken away from the brood at about the seventh week can form strong ties with both humans and other dogs but one removed from a litter when only a few days old and raised by hand will become an almost human dog with so little interest in other dogs that it may be unable to breed when it comes to dog's estate. A pup handled a lot at the right time, as I was, not only becomes more docile but learns faster than an isolated pup and is healthier because it is more resistant to stress.

My mistress and I quickly became devoted to each other and I suppose that I came to regard her as my mother. She, of course, soon became imprinted on me, regarding me, perhaps, almost as a child. Then sadly, after nearly two years of fun together, she decided to move to Australia and so we had to part, a situation in which I had no say. That is one aspect of the canine predicament – the uncertainty of the future over which we have no control. A change of home and ownership can be quite traumatic. Fortunately, we don't have the kind of mind that worries about the distant future, taking each minute as it comes.

Though my mistress did not know it, there was a couple not far away who were desperately looking for a dog. They were deeply distressed by the unexpected death of their favourite, a Rhodesian ridgeback, another properly proportioned dog which they had reared from puppyhood, and, never having been without a dog, they were in urgent need of a replacement. They sorely missed the intrusion of a well-loved, velvety snout, which can be so comforting, especially as they had been used to two dogs and sometimes even four.

By one of those strange things that happen in the countryside, which has its own means of communication, each heard of the other and were brought together, with me in attendance, one Friday evening. The couple lived in a village, called Kintbury, in

Berkshire, in a nice house next to the church. That suited me for I could never be a dog about town. While most of you choose to live in cities you have made them into nightmares of high-rise buildings where people live like battery chickens with so little territory and identity that the displacement behaviour of crime and vandalism is inevitable. The entire environment there seems to be a fearful mess, from what I have seen of it on my odd visits to London and other big cities. In fact, I don't see much difference between a big town and a zoo. A town is all right for alley cats, which can escape to the tiles, but not for dogs.

My entry into my new life was auspicious, perhaps uniquely so. The man who was to become my Chap was being interviewed on television when we arrived for our own interview with him. It was a recorded conversation about spies and as there was nobody else to answer the door it had to be interrupted, to the annoyance, I believe, of the television crew. Anyway I soon made up for it. The TV men wanted a shot of the Chap walking his dog through the churchyard to introduce the interview. As his dog had died I was able to act as stand-in. Though I would deny being a publicity hound, I performed very ably and little did I know that, in my small way, I would become a TV caninity, for I have been on several times since in similar circumstances, even on foreign stations. My photograph has also appeared in newspapers – even on the front page! So right from the start I brought him luck. There is a lot of nonsense talked about luck and the biggest is that black cats are the best for bringing it. Chocolate Labradors beat them out of sight!

Once the TV incident was over and the crew had packed up and gone I didn't care much what the couple looked like. In the dog world, where there is no fashion or standard of human beauty, handsome is as handsome does. For us beauty dwells with kindness.

The house seemed happy enough – we dogs can sense unhappiness – and there was a strong doggy smell about this couple, though I do not think that a human would have noticed it. But would we be compatible? That was the 64,000-bone question. They had never had a Labrador before, always having springer spaniels and ridgebacks, no doubt good dogs and true, but there must have been something prophetic about a doormat which the Chap had recently bought from a sports shop. It had a large dog woven into it and the only dog likeness the shop could provide was that of a Labrador. So, as my mistress remarked, before I even set paw in the house, there on the mat was 'Welcome' in the form of a silhouette which looked just like me. A good omen, if you believe in such things, as so many humans appear to do.

In my predicament I would need to transfer my affection to these new people from the girl who was, effectively, deserting me. Could I do it? Within minutes I had no doubts. There is a tide in the affairs of dog and I took it at the flood. The couple were as much in search of affection from a dog as I was from them. Dogs help to unify human relationships, especially for married couples whose children have grown up and left home. Grieving for their old dog, as they still were, this couple could not have been in a more receptive mood. I was the right dog in the right place at the right time.

Any dog's greatest social problem derives from the fact that it is totally at human mercy and can do nothing about it, beyond trying to please. So luck, which is the essence of uncertainty, plays a dominating role in our lives. Whether we get a kind, caring and, above all, understanding pack leader is a matter of luck and I certainly fell on my paws that day.

So far as the Chap was concerned I quickly saw that I could become his Dog Friday, and take him over to some extent. His wife looked affectionate, too, though she would probably stand less nonsense. She was clearly going to be the senior manager as far as my basic welfare would be concerned. There is an ashtray in one of the loos saying, 'The opinions expressed by the husband in this house are not necessarily those of the management', so, no doubt, I am right in thinking of her as the Boss.

Fortunately for me, with one recent exception, they had always had bitches – a word about which I am not too happy since it is used to imply an offensive woman and female dogs are rarely, if ever, that way. On the contrary, we are made and live for affection – giving it and receiving it. As one of your poets might have said, had he been more attuned to the canine world, 'Man's love is of man's life a thing apart. 'Tis bitch's whole existence.' As a female herself, the Boss appreciates that fully and my being a bitch worked strongly in my favour.

After little more than an exchange of delighted looks they bought me, cash on the nail, and the bargain hand-shake meant there was no going back on it. It had been love at first sight, as I have heard them say many times since, though in my case it had been more love at first sniff. I do not think it an exaggeration to use the word 'love'. When we love somebody we feel happiness in their company and sadness in separation. I am certainly capable of both feelings about this couple and I know that they fret if we are apart for long. Anyway, it was what my Chap calls a 'mutation moment', one of those sudden events which changes a whole life – his as well as mine.

As pack animals, both dogs and humans need to receive affection on a regular basis and need to give it. This is the fundamental reason why we get on so well together – our emotional requirements are the same. A display of affection imparts a sense of belonging and of security and these feelings, which are essential to our and your happiness, need reinforcing every day. In the wild I would get my share of affection from the rest of the pack but as an only dog in a household, which I have been ever since I left Devon, I have been entirely dependent on humans for my share. Our dependence and therefore our trust have to be total. We have no alternative. Humans do have an alternative – other members of their own pack, usually their family. What I cannot stand, what really hurts me, more than punishment, is rejection, even for a short time. That is why I love to stay close and to be noticed and touched. It is a mutual pleasure providing affectionate feelings to those making the fuss. (If you think about it, each day of the dog-man relationship is a miracle of mutual accommodation to each other's needs. No other creature approaches us in that capacity – certainly not the cat, which maintains a stubborn independence.)

It would be nice to have a canine pal to play with but there are compensations in being an only dog – as 80 per cent of us are in Britain. One is automatically top dog and gets more attention.

I didn't really realize that my young mistress was stepping out of my life but I was soon so engrossed with this new couple and in forging a survival bond with them that I quickly forgot all about her. Sad, perhaps, but then that's life and we must make the best of it. Maybe she will come back and see me one day when she has finished walking upside down.

My Chap, who is quite old but young at heart, turned out to be a retired 'news-hound' – a happy coincidence that should offer something in common. Further, he was continuing to earn his living as an author who might be induced to transcribe my ideas into English. As some poet nearly said, 'Fortune comes tumbling into some dogs' laps.'

I have already alluded to some of the Chap's oddities, which always seem to be more pronounced in the elderly. It was a sea-change from such a young mistress but there are decided advantages in having an old pack leader. Having no outside business to go to he is always around.

I watch carefully what he puts on in the morning. Suits are bad news for dogs. Usually, though, he wears his ropey old working clothes, which the Boss hates, saying they make him look like an old tramp (with which I agree). He won't throw anything away until it is worn out but old clothes are an excellent sign for me because they signify two things – he is not going to London and he will probably take me down to the river fishing some time for a couple of hours or so. He still spends far too much time working in his study for my taste but I do my best to ensure that we are rarely seen one without the other.

The Boss has also, belatedly, become an author and she has her study, too, which is very convenient if the Chap's gets too noisy, which it sometimes does when he is playing his radiogram, as he usually is when he is working.

So we all learn something about each other every day, as I think this book will show.

3 Territorial Imperatives

Breathes there the dog with soul so dead
That never to herself hath said
This is my own, my native patch.

Once I had been handed over, along with my pedigree form, I belonged to the Chap and the Boss in human law but that is not the way I look at it. Far from being adopted as an extension of the family, it was I who accepted the family as members of my pack. If more dog 'owners' appreciated this their relationships with us would be more solidly based. It's not me and them. It's we three. A pack of three – one for all and all for one, the pack right or wrong. Those are the guidelines for the relationship. Like a successful marriage, it is a partnership, a team in which we have trust and faith in each other. That is the realistic basis for the bond between dog and man. Some dogs make the mistake of treating their owners like animals when, at all times, we must remember that they are only human.

My faith in my Chap is absolute and when he leaves me to guard the house he shows his faith in me but it is because the house is also my property that I defend it. I will have a go at anybody who appears to threaten it or its human owners because the house and all its contents, living and still, form my den and the garden and area around it are my territory – my patch. Just as the wolf defends her den and the ground around it so do I. When I confront a stranger it may look as though I am defending my Chap and the Boss. If I am, that is incidental. I am defending my own territory and my property of which they are part. They think that I belong to them but I regard them as belonging to me and I don't like any outside interference with my possessions, whether they be dead bones or living persons. Any jealousy I display is much more likely to be in defence of my human possessions than a mark of excessive affection. That may sound unromantic but it is realistic and, as I have already said, that is what we dogs are and need to be.

In our wolf days, our territories were staked out and marked by scent posts – stumps, trees, rocks, which the males visited, reinforced with their own scent, both liquid and solid, and examined for the trademark of any intruder. It was, of course, easier for a pack to mark out and defend a large territory than for a single dog. The liquid marks lasted about a month before they needed to be reinforced while, to a perceptive nose, a solid offering spoke volumes about its perpetrator for even longer. This 'Kilroy was here' process is still carried out diligently by dogs which are allowed to roam freely. I can never be paw-loose and fancy free because we have a completely walled garden from which I cannot wander. I suppose that to a large extent I am caged but then so are you for the greater part of your waking time – in your office, factory, kitchen or car. Anyway, I do not think I would go any distance without my Chap. I would be wondering what he was up to in my absence and what I was missing! If this book makes me famous there will be a further reason for not wandering. I might be dognapped and held to ransom.

A dog's house is her castle. I don't want to fight for it if I can avoid it, though I have the necessary equipment in my mouth. Usually, all I need to do is to give a good savage-sounding bark to let people know that the area is occupied and will be defended if necessary. I have a deep and quite frightening bark for a female and I find reason – or excuse – to let rip with it a few times every day. Every dog is entitled to its woofs and it is no bad thing to remind the villagers and anyone else who might be passing that there is a sharp dog on the premises. Like you, we are a vocal species and if you can't bark in Berkshire where can you bark?

I have to confess, however, that when I run so bravely to the back gates it is because I know that they are shut and there will not be any real confrontation with either dog or man. On rare occasions, when the Chap has forgotten to close the gates after bringing his car in, I have run out and found myself face to face with a passing dog. We have both been surprised to the point of embarrassment because, all the way back to our wolf days, the objective is to state our claims without physical conflict. Obvious possession of territory is usually accepted with little hassle and even the smallest dog can usually see off a canine intruder. After all, biting is no good to any of us if we can avoid it. We save that for our food and we are not cannibals, though some of your lot used to be.

Most dogs bark back, ferociously, when they can spot me through the gap at the bottom of the gate and know that I cannot get out. There is one that comes with its master each morning to pick up the news-papers and, invariably, we have a good barking match because I lie in wait for her. It's the same if we meet in public and are both on leads. But if we meet when we are free we simply ignore each other, like two women might cut each other if they meet in the street.

Of course, some dogs are savage by nature and it is the over-dominant dog which tends to bite a stranger from an alien pack, human or canine. Others become savage because of the way they are treated, usually by being kept tied up, sometimes cruelly. They develop inordinate attachment to their pitifully restricted territory. Having so little that they can call their own they defend it excessively against all comers – sometimes including their owners. All too often, I fear, this reaction is exploited in order to make a dog savage so that it will deter intruders. Farmers are common offenders, sometimes leaving a dog on a long chain for days on end.

Happily I am never tied up and can come and go in and out of the house from the garden through swinging dog-doors. That way I can deal with all intruders, night and day, including cats and, on one occasion, a large hedgehog which somehow managed to get in through the gap under the wooden gates. I quickly sniffed it out and, though I did not fancy picking it up, the Chap removed it smartly to the churchyard from where it had probably come to feed on the slugs, in which my patch is rather rich.

My territory is big enough. Being free from acquisitiveness (except for food) we do not crave more property for the sake of having it, like so many humans do. Indeed, the penalties your laws impose are sometimes greater for assault on your property than for violence against the person. Too much property would be a nuisance to us and we are not interested in status symbols so we don't want a bigger territory than we need. We prefer as easy a life as we can get. In the wild our territories would be small when food was abundant. So, now that a lucky dog like myself has been relieved of the need to hunt for food, my territorial requirements are quite modest – just a spot to call my own and big enough to enable me to go through the motions of defending it without too much effort.

My need for possessions is also modest, while most humans go on acquiring material goods, often just for the sake of having them. All I need is a bowl, a bed, a collar and lead and two or three toys, like a rubber bone, a ball, and one of those things called a pull. I might stockpile a few real bones but the mania for collecting seems to be exclusively human, apart from magpies, which some people resemble. Collectors claim that the search for objects to acquire helps to fulfil the hunting instinct but, if that is so, why haven't I got it?

We divide our territory into different areas – for sleeping and eating (if we have a bone) with an area for what you call spending pennies and tuppences. You, of course do the same and, since we thought of it first, I wonder if you copied us. Even if you have to live in a bed-sitter you instinctively divide it up into different areas for different purposes.

It really is remarkable how wonderfully we have adapted to each other's ways. We are from a very different ethnic culture and, though there are some awkward customers and delinquents among us, we have conformed to your requirements to an astonishing degree. The motorcar provides a good example. It could hardly be a more artificial mode of transport for us yet my Chap can't keep me out of it. I love to feel the wind on my nostrils through a half-open car window as we cruise along. I regard the Chap and the Boss as my chauffeurs and they even hold the door open to enable me to get in and out and close it after me, as good chauffeurs should. The window is never completely open any more because of an incident which occurred on the M6 motorway. We were cruising along, with the Boss driving, when suddenly a wad of documents which my Chap had been reading was sucked out of his hands by the slip stream and blown all over the road. They contained confidential information, to do with some intelligence book he was planning, but there was no way he could stop and pick them up in all that traffic. So

41

on we pressed hoping that nobody would ever find and read them. There's never a dull moment with my Chap!

I suppose I am taking a risk putting my nose out of the windows because they are electric and if they went up suddenly I might be in painful trouble. There is a back-seat safety belt but I am never put in it. Perhaps I ought to be because nearly five stones of me being propelled forwards at 60 miles an hour would not be pleasant for any of us if it hit the driver or a front-seat passenger. Still, risks are part of the fun of life and nothing is going to keep me out of the car.

Thank heavens I am not car sick. I have heard of some dogs who are sick as soon as they get into a car, which, understandably, they come to hate. It is the sight of the countryside flashing by that seems to do it and dark goggles might help if dogs could be induced to wear them.

I have only hated the car once, and then only for a few minutes. This was the occasion when, as one of his so-called behavioural experiments, the Chap took me through the local garage's robot car-wash to see how I would react. I must say that it was anything but pleasant – all that water and those great, hairy rollers coming towards me. I was curious at first but once the rollers began to bang on the roof and windows and the light went dim it was all too much like a thunderstorm. Fortunately, the Chap and the Boss were close by so I did not panic but just curled up until the ordeal was over. The only thing it taught them was that before going into a car-wash it is wise to stow the aerial. In their concentration on what I might or might not do they had forgotten what to do themselves. The aerial was snapped off so the joke was finally on them.

The car is, in fact, the nearest thing I have to a kennel, what Americans call a dog-house, and when it is in our garage, which opens on to the garden,

42

my Chap leaves the rear door open all day so that I can get in and out. The back seat is very comfortable for a nap. It also means that my Chap cannot go anywhere without I know it and probably get taken. I am never 'in the dog-house' as a punishment, though I am sometimes consigned to the car when the house is full of guests.

Of course, the car is part of my territory whenever I am in it and wherever it is because, to me, it is another den. That's why I bark so fiercely at other dogs or anyone who comes near it and might try to get in. I never bark when I am on a train and other people try to get into our carriage because I know that it is not mine.

When I am in the car I reckon I am more effective than any alarm system. Nobody is going to nick the radio or the groceries but I am not just protecting them as such but my territory as a whole. By and large, however, I get bored when I am taken shopping and always have to be left in the car. There are far too many places these days where dogs are not allowed. Through the fault of the media and politicians, with their scare stories, everybody is far too germ-conscious and the whole fear that dogs are 'dirty' has become grossly exaggerated. I can see a reason for keeping male dogs out of shops because they start staking out scent posts, but not bitches. Fortunately, as a former biologist, my Chap has no hang-ups about bacteria, which have always been around and always will be, and takes a balanced view. I have so often noticed with humans that what they fear is what they don't understand. It is odd that, with one exception, while there are so many things that I do not understand I am not frightened of anything I have seen or experienced so far – at least, not for long. The exception is any vet's surgery. The moment I sniff the air there I get the shivers and my teeth begin to chatter. I suppose it harks back to the time when, as a puppy, I was kicked by a horse and had to be stitched up. I do not doubt that the vet means well but so does your dentist and you don't relish going there, do you?

4 Beauty is in the Nose of the Beholder

*Smelled scents are sweet
but those unsmelled are sweeter*

The canine predicament is much more down to earth than yours – literally. The world looks and smells very different eighteen inches off the ground. Get down on your knees and test it, on the carpet, in a field or on the pavement, like my Chap has done with down-to-dog determination, to the amused astonishment of onlookers. Our environment is a world swimming in odours which are hardly discernible five feet higher. We take the nose to the scent while, standing aloft, as you all do, the scent has to come to your nose, sometimes being held close to it before you can discern it – another disadvantage of walking on only two legs.

Even the best-swept carpet smells of all manner of things. The pavements, roads, and walls give off a variety of smells which you scarcely notice but we cannot avoid and which make a walk so much more meaningful for us. It is not just the exercise or the joy of running that makes us pester you to take us out. The fields, trees and hedgerows are equally awash with scents. Grass may have no smell to you until it is cut but, with our noses so close to it, we detect a rich aroma at all times. Gardeners get a slight nasal glimpse of the smell of soil when they bend down and put their noses near to it but it reeks to us at all times, especially when all the microscopic fungi which live in it start fruiting after rain.

That is also the first smell of spring – when everything is bursting through the soil. For me, the seasons are as much a matter of scent as of temperature and light. In summer the leaves of the plants and trees each have a distinctive smell, apart from the flowers. You don't smell leaves closely but in autumn, even at the height of your noses, you cannot fail to detect the scent of the fallen leaves. Imagine the strength of it to my nose! In winter when scents are locked in by frost, ice and snow their absence has positive meaning for me.

We dogs use nose and ears first and sight last. When you offer us something with which we are not thoroughly familiar we use the nose to examine it as you would use your eyes. You get an eyeful of a scene: we get a noseful. While you might say, 'As I see the situation . . .' I would say, 'As I smell it . . .' or when you say, 'Oh, I see,' to mean that you understand something, I would say, 'Oh, I smell.' Such is the predominance of scent in our lives.

So, it follows that just as you like to stand and stare and admire a view so we like to stand and savour the scents. Humans can have no real appreciation of how marvellous a scent can be or they wouldn't try to drag us away when we are savouring a particularly sensuous aroma. 'What is this life if, it is meant, we have no time to stand and scent!'

When my Chap and I go for a walk he can see what is there but I can also detect what has been there. To us things are far more often in smell than in view. Some of the scents reaching us on the breeze may be from distant sources but are still of interest in building up a smell picture of the situation. That is why the wind on the heath is so specially delectable to us and I so enjoy having my nose out of the window as the car speeds along. It is the smells I am interested in, rather than the scenery.

When you discern a strong smell, which is usually unpleasant if you remark on it, multiply it a hundred times or more to imagine how it strikes us. And I do mean 'strikes'. The particles arising from the smell source assail the olfactory sense cells which are located not just on the inside of my nose, like yours are, but also on the outside, which is why it is usually moist. By trapping airborne particles my wet nose, with its mobile nostrils, enables me to detect the slightest scents. No smell particles can affect either of us until they are dissolved in nasal liquid – a hark-back to the distant days when our extinct ancestors were aquatic creatures, fish or something like fish.

While you humans tend to bestialize our noses by calling them 'snouts', your nose is still the dominant feature of your face and, in the Chap's case, outstandingly so. When he was studying the markings on my nose through his big Sherlock Holmes magnifying glass he didn't realize how huge and how peculiar his own looked from my side of it. Yet the actual olfactory area inside his nose is only about 5-square centimetres, little bigger than a postage stamp, while mine is about 150-square centimetres, getting on for half the size of this page. He has about 5 million olfactory sense cells: I have about 250 million! It would be a major hardship for me if my nose was blocked by a cold like his is so often, and probably yours, but dogs don't get colds.

It is not just the canine nose that has it. That part of the brain concerned with smelling is much better developed in the dog than in the human, where the available space inside the skull is concentrated on vision. When you close your eyes half the surface of your brain shuts down, such is the dominance of your vision, but the effect on my brain is much smaller and I can't shut my nose, which would have a similar result.

Because of the domination of our smell sense, our brains make a quite different picture of what you see with your eyes. We don't see you as you see us. Our concept of you is a mixture of sight and smell – an aura, if you like, and that is what we welcome back so rapturously when you return home – your odour as well as the sight of you.

As you retain visual images like photographs in your memories, we retain scent pictures, what might be called smellographs, in our minds. We can conjure up old smells in our memories and in our dreams. On occasion we may experience a smell hallucination like you 'see things'. Oh the sheer delight of smells! If only I had the ability to paint some of my favourite smell pictures – the things I smell in my mind's nose!

It is because we are motivated by some smells to which you are totally oblivious that you cannot understand some of the things we do, like barking when you can't hear anything or becoming restless for no obvious reason. Sometimes when I scrabble at a carpet the Boss thinks I am just being destructive but I know that there is something interesting underneath it, something that may be very small. The trouble is that our inherited standards are so different. By the standards of our culture, what to you is foul smelling, such as an over-ripe bone or even a long-dead sheep, to us is a fragrance to be savoured slowly and deeply, like you savour the bouquet of wine. It can be so attractive that we might even like to anoint ourselves with it, as you use perfumes.

Most of the smells which interest us, like bones, raw meat and birds, are deeply rooted in our past but we are eternally grateful to you for a few, among which my favourites are meat dishes being prepared, toast, which always sends me racing downstairs, chocolate, and, of course, the smell of those humans whom we love.

However, humans have little conscious idea what we have to put up with in the way of smells which we could do without, for some of the scents you enjoy are objectionable to us. As you are blinded by light we can be saturated by smells such as those concoctions the Boss puts in her bath. That horrible stuff she sprays on her hair is another. The Chap calls the loo spray 'the greatest civilizing instrument of recent times' but I detest it. Petrol is another hate, though there is an additional reason why I dislike it. My Chap uses it to make a tick dislodge itself when I have picked one up on the Common and, while it quickly does the trick and I should be grateful, it does sting.

We sometimes smell strongly to you, especially when we are wet. 'That dog smells very doggy', the Boss is inclined to say, with some distaste. Well, what else would I smell like? Anyway, you smell manny to us all the time. Human sweat contains butyric acid, the substance which makes rancid butter smell the way it does, but we get used to it. We have to and we put up with it without complaint. (We could move away with one of those 'if your best friend won't tell you' gestures but we don't – at least not obviously.) We can, in fact, detect butyric acid when it is so dilute that it would have to be a million times stronger before you could smell it. It just seems to be a happy coincidence – or it could be destiny – that the substance which we can detect in such small amounts is the one that the human body secretes all the time and which enables us to keep you in smell or to find and follow you. Dogs, like St Bernards, which have been trained to find people buried by avalanches can smell a man ten feet down in thick snow. One Austrian dog taken out to look for its missing master refused to move from a certain spot in deep snow, staying there for three days until rescuers decided that they had better dig and, miraculously, discovered the man just alive. Greater love hath no dog, except for several cases in which dogs have starved to death sitting faithfully by their master's remains!

The human body exhales so many other odours that there is an infinite number of different mixtures so that each person has a scent as individual as a fingerprint, a fact which detectives may be able to use one day to convict criminals, if research, in which dogs are assisting, proves to be successful. My Chap may look very different in a smart business suit but the body inside it smells the same and I could scent him out, blindfolded, across the proverbial crowded room.

By their nature, some people are easier on the nose than others. (Usually those who are not cannot understand why we are reluctant to be friendly.) Further, I can tell you that individual scent changes according to mood. Sweating is linked with the hormone system and when the glands react, as they do at great speed in various stressful situations, so do the sweat glands. I know immediately when a stranger dislikes dogs because his odour changes the moment he sees me. It can either be the odour of aversion or the odour of fear. The latter can sometimes be so strong that it induces a savage dog to attack the person emitting it, which is why some people seem prone to being bitten. By contrast, I can sense dog lovers the moment they enter the room as well as poseurs – those who pretend to like us but don't really. I can also sense people who dislike my Chap and, automatically, I dislike them. Love me love my man! (While a few dogs are born distrustful of everybody, people would be well advised to take care with anyone whom a normally friendly dog dislikes on sight.)

Human odour is also affected by diet – even your poor nose can detect the garlic-eater – by age and by sickness. In response to the various germs which attack the human body, odours are produced which are so different that trained dogs might be able to diagnose illnesses much earlier than doctors, though I do not think it has been tried yet. The idea does offer some enchanting prospects though – call in Dr Dog for a second opinion! I wonder if he would be required to wear a mask and gown. This is not quite as crazy as it may sound. Hospitals are being encouraged to have dogs in the wards to cheer up long-stay patients and give them an interest and I imagine that they are subjected to special cleanliness precautions.

Babies and young children have a smell which instinctively alerts me to the fact that I must be gentle with them, as I am with puppies. There is even a family smell so that when grandchildren and other relatives whom I had not met came to visit, I knew they belonged and gave them a special welcome as occasional members of the pack. If the species smell – what makes you smell human and me doggy – is inherited through the genes, why shouldn't there be a family smell?

While we enjoy the natural scent of dog you are ashamed of your scent and do what you can to conceal it with anti-perspirant sprays, soap, perfumes, dentifrices and mouthwashes. But they don't fool us. We can still smell you clearly through it all.

Some owners even subject their dogs to anti-odour sprays. My Chap had a friend whose wife used to treat his shooting spaniel with a perfume called Tweed. The dog hated it and, while the scent lasted, it made him a menace in the field because other gun dogs were more interested in the novelty of his smell than in the pheasants.

Because of the way we have been selected, both by nature and by humans, we Labradors are particularly noted for our sense of smell. We make the most reliable of all gun dogs and can be trained to detect things like explosives and drugs hidden in luggage and even dry rot in floorboards under thick carpets. My nose is so sensitive that I can detect the odour of meat through seven thicknesses of paper. I can scent a man or another dog from a distance of 500 yards or even longer if the wind is blowing my way. In our early days together the Chap tried me out in a way which was, quite frankly, insulting. He hid a piece of chocolate in one hand and a soya-bean pellet in the other. Of course, I never made a mistake. To my nose the chocolate reeked out, 'Here I am!'

Always one for experiments he has repeatedly stooped to smell the tips of twigs and bramble stems which engage my rapt attention on our walks because, at some time, they have been anointed by passing dogs. He has never been able to detect the slightest scent of anything. He has even blindfolded himself and plugged his ears with cotton wool to test how well he could find his way about a room or the garden just by smell. Of course, he got nowhere while I would have had no problems. While humans are almost completely dependent on their eyes for finding their way about I can 'hoover' my way around. I can dog a man's footsteps but he can't man mine. I can follow my Chap's trail even when it is criss-crossed by others, as we have proved many times. Moreover I could follow my own scent back home if I was lost on a walk. You can't even recognize your scent – not even when it is strong enough for other people to do so.

In experiments dogs have been able to detect the body odour of one person when it was deliberately mixed up with the scent of another. Some dogs can even detect a difference in the trail of identical twins, though I have never had the opportunity to try. There is a sound biological reason for this ability. Way back in time we had to be able to follow the trail of one particular animal, like a deer or a moose, because our only hope of catching it was to run it down to exhaustion, our endurance being greater. If the pack kept picking up the trail of a fresh animal we would never have had any dinner. That, of course, was the reason that you used us for hunting, and still do, being devoid of such ability yourselves.

There are some days when the scent is easy for us to follow and others when it is very difficult. It depends on humidity, frost and the wind. Scent is good when the soil or grass is moist and on foggy days or at night when evaporation is slow. It is usually poor when the smell particles are quickly dried off by a hot sun or a strong wind and when they are held fast by ice or hard frost. As you can imagine, heavily manured land does not help because it provides too much competition.

On days when there is little scent our situation is rather like yours would be in a thick fog. Where there is a strong crosswind we do not follow the actual trail but keep a few feet leeward of it. Whatever the conditions, we press on somehow until we succeed. Our dogged determination is a byword in your language.

Incidentally, though we are among the best, we are not the world's greatest smellers. My sense of smell is not nearly as sensitive as a wolf's. The wild wolf's brain is about 25 per cent bigger than an Alsatian's of similar size because domestication eventually reduces the size of the brain in any animal. However, it is those parts of the brain connected with smell and other senses vital to the wolf's survival, and which we no longer need quite so much, which are bigger. So having a smaller brain does not mean that we are less intelligent.

Even the wild wolf is beaten by the salmon, which can smell its way from the far Atlantic back to the very creek of the river in which it was born. But you could hardly use a salmon for tracking a criminal, guiding a blind person or detecting dope in baggage at London Airport, like you can use a domesticated wolf, which is, basically, what I am.

5 Seeing – at Hem-line Level

The light that lies in bitch's eyes

My eyes look almond-shaped, though they are really spherical like yours, and they are bigger than yours in proportion to my body. Because I can run at such speed, my eyes must have a high resolving power to keep things in sharp focus, which is why they are so big, just as a horse's are. I have amber-brown irises and round pupils and I do not show much of the whites. When you view a close object your pupils contract but mine dilate. I have short eyelashes on the top lids and also have the protection of a third eyelid, which comes over from the inner side and can cover three quarters of each eye. All you have in the way of a third lid is a useless bump called a caruncle – that little pink spot in the inner corner.

I blink my lids quite a lot to keep my eyes lubricated, like you do, and occasionally I appear to flutter them, which the Chap says is a well-known female stratagem.

On my eyebrows I have a few black whiskers which are extremely sensitive to touch and I wonder if yours were, originally. Otherwise yours don't seem to serve much purpose apart from possibly preventing sweat from getting into your eyes. My Chap's eyebrows are very slight and he does not seem to have suffered much inconvenience.

In most mammals, including you, each eye is completely surrounded by bone but ours are not. The outside border of each of our eyes is protected only by a ligament, which you can feel. It means that our eyes do not have such strong protection from injury as yours but it enables our jaws to have more play in seizing food, which was especially important when we hunted prey. You can never have everything, can you? There's always some penalty to pay for an advantage, whatever your species.

I can't roll my eyes upwards in my sockets like you can but, then, you do not make much use of that to see but only to express disgust, which I rarely feel.

As I have already said, my eyes are placed more on the sides of my head than yours which gives me a wider field of vision but means that my stereoscopic sight is not so good. So, when I want to pinpoint something, like a mouse in the grass or one of those huge spiders scurrying across the carpet, I cock my head on one side to fix it better with one eye. I know it looks cute but that is not why I do it.

My Chap cannot creep up on me when we are larking about in the garden because my eyes give me a total field of vision of 250 degrees. His eyes are placed so frontally that, without moving his whole head, his field is only 180 degrees. So I can creep up on him and often do. It does mean, though, that, with less binocular vision, I am not so good at judging distance or seeing stationary objects as he is. I could not easily recognize you at a distance if you stood still. You could be a bush.

I understand that your stereoscopic vision is probably a hangover from the days when your ancestors lived in trees because they needed it for swinging from branch to branch. At least nobody can say to us that we are just down from the trees!

With my eyes only eighteen inches off the ground, my horizons are so much closer than yours that the world looks very different, as you can easily appreciate for yourself if you get down to our level on your hands and knees either in a field or on a pavement. On rocky ground or where there are hummocks our vision is even more restricted and we have to rely on our sense of smell to tell us what is round the corner. It is no coincidence that those breeds of dog which have been bred for coursing by sight – the gaze-hounds like the greyhound, saluki and borzoi – have long legs and necks to give them a better view.

We don't often see you face to face because we are usually looking up at you while you look down on us, giving us a psychological disadvantage, as a man does when he wants to dominate you at an interview and sits you in a lower chair than he has. Unless we are on a chair or a bed your face is mostly chin to us and not at all what you see in a mirror. When we try to communicate it is as though you were trying to talk to a crow in a tree. We recognize you by the whole of your body and especially by your legs for our world is dominated by legs.

Of course, we like to see more of you, which is why we like to jump up, a mark of curiosity as well as of affection which gets me into trouble especially if I happen to ladder somebody's stockings.

Sometimes we are accused of running right over something which you can see easily from your high vantage point, but we are not being stupid, we just can't see it from our height.

There is another huge difference which you need to take into account. We are colour blind. What you see as contrasting colours we see only as black, white and various shades of grey, as you do when watching non-colour TV. So the brightly coloured pheasant which is so obvious to you lying on green grass is, to us, a grey object lying on a grey background and is by no means as easy to see. Nature has denied us one of the joys of your life while at the same time greatly improving the camouflage of creatures we might prey on. The brown rabbit or hare in a field is difficult enough for you to see if it remains still but imagine what it is like to us – a grey creature on grey ground. Even my own chocolate colour just looks greyish-black to me when I lick my fur to keep myself clean.

When my Chap plays the matador game with me, shaking a towel so that I charge in, the colour does not matter. It is the movement that attracts both me and the bull, which is also colour blind. If I was in earnest I might be the more dangerous opponent because, unlike the bull, I charge with my eyes open. No female would be daft enough to charge with her eyes shut. I am told that even enraged cows keep them open.

Why did Nature land us with such a disadvantage as blindness to colour? The answer lays way back in our evolution when we hunted almost exclusively in the dusk, darkness and early dawn when colours were unimportant to us and now we are stuck with it forever. A pity, when our world is your world and so multi-coloured, especially in your homes. I wonder if our lack of colour experience is why snow excites us so much though it could be a hark-back to our wolf days, in which snow played such a part.

In dim light, when colour fades, you can begin to appreciate what the world looks like to us all the time but I can see much better than you can then. Many people see very poorly in dim light when everything looks grey and blends together. They suffer from what eye specialists call night myopia, which is a problem of the eye muscles, and some see so little that they are almost blind then. I, too, only see greys in the twilight but because of the structure of my eyes I can see almost as clearly then as in daylight, and even under a sky lit only by stars my vision is still good. The retinas of my eyes have more of the structures called rods, which are very sensitive to light and my pupils expand enormously at night. So a comparatively small amount of light falling on them produces quite a bright picture in my brain. When I stand at one end of my garden in the dark and my Chap (or an intruder) stands at the other I can see every movement he makes though he cannot see me at all. Of course, no creature can see in complete darkness but that is extremely rare, and even then my nose works as well as ever.

Behind each of my retinas there is a layer of tissue which glistens and reflects light back into the eye, giving me further assistance in dim light. That is why my eyes sometimes appear to shine in the dark.

Primitive man did not need any of these built-in advantages because he slept at night but the wolf and primitive dog did because they hunted at night as well as by day. When man and dog began to hunt in partnership their different visual and nasal advantages dovetailed to give them the best of both worlds.

In addition to just seeing there is the question of recognition. We do that mostly by smell but eyes play their part, though in a different way from yours. We can remember visually, though not in colour, and to nothing like the extent that you can. For example, while you can easily recognize a male dog by sight, if you can get a rear view, I have to scent him. I cannot recognize a dog on the television screen by its appearance, though I might respond to a bark. There has to be much more to the concept of 'dog' than a flat, odourless image for it to be accepted by me as another dog. It is the same with a human. My Chap appeared on television recently and the Boss tried to get me to watch him. I recognized his voice and looked behind the set to see if he was there but the picture of him meant nothing. It was flat and there was no smell.

For the same reason, objects in a mirror mean little to me. I am momentarily interested in the movement of my reflection but I do not recognize it as me or as a dog at all. Perhaps it is just as well. Otherwise I would become like the females of your species and spend too much time looking at myself.

Self-love is not one of your more laudable characteristics and I suspect that it arises from your feelings of insecurity, which I don't have. Being too aware of all your circumstances and what the future might hold, you need to reassure yourself, constantly, that you are rather special – particularly if, in your heart of hearts, you know that you are not.

Movement is immensely important to us in recognizing things and we are very sensitive to objects in motion. I cannot spot a rabbit sitting motionless, even ten yards away if it is down wind of my nose, but am immediately interested if it moves. Greyhounds, which do not have such a good sense of smell, will even chase a mechanical hare if it moves as fast as a real one.

While we can spot movements better than a man can, our long-distance vision is not so good. About 500 yards is our limit for a stationary object, with half a mile the limit for something moving. When we do our parlour tricks to satisfy our human masters and mistresses we are often taking far more notice of their unconscious movements than of their verbal commands, as I will explain in my chapter on Communication.

Like yours, our eyesight fades as we age and many dogs are destroyed because they have become blind. There is no good reason for it. Most blind dogs can cope and lead happy lives provided their noses remain active, as they generally do. A dog that is blind from birth, as some are, manages far better than congenitally blind humans because of the predominance of the smell sense. Indeed, a dog without a sense of smell would be far worse off than a blind dog. Blindness usually comes on gradually, so a dog has time to adapt to its new circumstances and make even greater use of its power of smell, like a sightless person's hearing becomes more acute. We cope so well that many dogs are blind, or nearly so, before their owners begin to notice it. In the wild state a blind dog might well have been killed in the interests of the pack's general survival but we have put that savagery behind us. So should you.

6 Listening In

Who in ears matches me?

Like yours, my real ears are inside my skull, and what you call my ears are just flaps protecting the entrances. The flaps are short, which makes them less sensitive to cold. Larger ears would be an advantage in a hot climate, as elephants' are, because they act as radiators for excess body heat, but we do not have many hot summers so I would rather have them short and certainly not long enough to get into my food. A wolf's ear flaps are stiff and erect, instead of being floppy like mine, and are better for hearing because they act like funnels for sound. An Alsatian has inherited that advantage but my ear flaps are easier to lie on and, while I can't prick them up much, they are better for keeping the dust out. I can flick them to get rid of a fly, using muscles which you still possess, showing that once, way back in time, you needed to prick up your ears. The best any of you can do with them now is to produce a minuscule waggle.

My ears are also very soft and velvety and give my Chap and the Boss tactile pleasure out of touching them, which also gives pleasure to me. Touching human ears does nothing for anybody.

The entrance to the business part of each of my ears which is buried in bone inside, is protected by hairs that keep out any curious insects. Then there is a lot of waxy stuff which acts like flypaper, so a flea wouldn't get far in my ear!

In addition to the actual hearing apparatus, which is remarkably like yours to look at, each of my inner ears contains what amounts to an automatic pilot. It has three little semicircular tubes, each set in a different plane of space so that, whatever dimension I move in, my brain can take note of it and make sure that I keep steady on my legs. Very ingenious! You have the same arrangement but I reckon that mine is more effective. When running at speed I can turn completely round on a sixpence (perhaps I should say a 20p coin now) without ever tipping over. One of the Chap's previous dogs, a spaniel called Skipper, had a defective automatic pilot and was inclined to stagger even when standing still.

Dozens of experiments have shown that our ears are much more sensitive than yours in many ways, especially to faint sounds. We can hear sounds which are too soft, too high or too low to be detected by the human ear unaided by instruments. We can also hear ultrasonic sounds which mean nothing at all to you. This was all very useful to our wolf ancestors who could hear soft footfalls in the snow and who listened for high-pitched ultrasounds made by rodents under the snow, as they do to this day.

As I have said, when we are told to stop barking because there is nothing there it is almost always because your ears are at fault. It is for this reason that dogs have sometimes been credited with sensing a ghost walking by in a room. All that the dog has done is to react to something, like a fox, for instance, walking outside, and has followed the slight sound with its head, even perhaps growling in the process.

Experiments also prove that we dogs are much superior to humans in picking out just where a nearby sound comes from. And we are better than men at judging the direction of a distant sound though not so good at judging how far away it is. When a distant gun goes off, as it often does round here, I can immediately sense its location and turn my head that way while the Chap is by no means sure of the direction. Scientists once put dogs in a hole in the ground and then rang bells from different points 25 yards away. The dogs could always detect the position of the bells but the scientists couldn't. No comment!

I can also detect minute differences in sounds. For example, I can recognize the footsteps of my Chap or the Boss through double glazing, which pre-empts scent. I can also distinguish between their car and anybody else's when they pull up outside the house. A lot of people park outside my Chap's study window and I take no notice of them. The sound of their cars means nothing to me. All this means, of course, that, like you, we store sound memories. For instance, when I hear the screech of the Chap's fishing reel I know that he is into a fish and I come running.

Experiments, which I regard as rather strange, have shown that we dogs have a super-human capacity to distinguish the intervals between sounds. A dog can tell the difference between a metronome beating at 100 times a minute and one beating at 102 or only 98, which is far beyond the capability of even the greatest musician. We can distinguish notes which are only one fifth the distance apart of two adjacent notes on a piano. We can detect a fraction of a tone which is beyond the capacity of the most well-tuned human ear. A pity we can't compose, though some dogs howl in an individual way which, I suppose, could be set to music.

All in all, we live in a much noisier world than you but, like you, our brains are able to ignore and blot out the sounds that mean nothing to us while remaining ever alert to those that do.

It is because we hear so well that some of us are frightened when shotguns are fired. Fortunately, I am not, which is just as well because gun-shyness seems to be inherited and dogs do not get over it. Because of the sensitivity of our ears thunder also sounds much louder to us and we can sense it in the distance long before you do. This is useful to the Chap if he spots my behaviour while we are out fishing. It is dangerous to fish with a carbon-fibre rod when there is lightning about so he gets advance warning. He once had a springer spaniel, called Honey, who ate her way through the wooden slats of a large window in her effort to escape when she had been left alone in a thunderstorm. I am not that hysterical and confess that I overdo my anxiety in order to get asked upstairs during a storm at night. Nevertheless, it is a hell of a din to us — far louder than it is to you.

Pheasants are greatly disturbed by thunder, too, and there are so many round our village that I can hear them crowing in the night the moment that they feel the first aerial vibrations of a coming storm.

I also hate the noise of the jet of the hot-air balloons which often come low over our village from a nearby launching ground. Pheasants don't like it either. My Chap was once at a shoot close by when a dozen balloons came low over the pheasant cover and ruined the drive.

When the Chap blows his little hunting horn close to me to amuse his grandchildren I can be guaranteed to bark rather frenziedly but that is mainly because I know that it is a joke at my expense and we dogs do not like to be ridiculed. A certain degree of dignity is important to any pack animal and no fun should be at the expense of it.

The clackety-clack of the printer attached to my Chap's word processor also sends me running, but that is partly due to my realization that it means he is going to be busy for quite a while so I had better look elsewhere for attention.

When I am in my Chap's study I have to listen to music, day in, day out. He reckons that a house that is filled with great music must be a happy house. I suppose he could be right but he never plays the opera written about my namesake, the Queen of Carthage, and her goings-on with a chap called Aeneas. The music is always classical so it is not deafening like that pop music which we sometimes hear in parked cars and blares so loudly that I can hardly hear myself bark. In both cases I just ignore it. All it means to me when the Chap starts to listen to music is that we are not going out. The sweet song of my friend George, the canary who lives in the conservatory and matches my yellow collar, is much preferable, though he is rather prone, these days, to do what my Chap calls 'his strong silent bird act'.

I like it when the radio is left on if the couple go out and leave me. But it is not the music that I appreciate – just the noise, whatever it is. It makes me feel that I am not entirely alone which, I suppose, is half the reason that humans like the radio on when they are on their own in the house.

Like any intelligent dog I have learned to recognize certain spoken commands and other words. I know my name, 'sit', 'stay', 'leave it', 'come out', 'go to your place', 'shut up' and so on. With many words it is not so much what the Chap and the Boss say as how they say it. There are various ways of shouting 'Dido' and I am in no doubt when they are praising me and when I am being told off.

Like fading eyesight, deafness is another symptom of canine ageing, as it is with you but, in the case of gun dogs, it is often inflicted by their masters. There is no doubt whatever that the regular use of a shotgun impairs human hearing and it is now customary for shooters to wear earplugs or earmuffs, called defenders. Loaders and wives standing near a shooter also wear them for protection. Gun dogs stand near their masters in the shooting field and it would be surprising if their ears were not affected. So how about ear-defenders for dogs? My Chap has tried me out with a pair of his. I did not object to them and they could easily be adapted to fit my head more comfortably. It is something we dogs should work on.

Water in the ears when we swim is also supposed to be a cause of deafness. Humans use earplugs to avoid it these days and perhaps dogs should be fitted with those, too, when we are sent in to retrieve something from water, though I imagine they would be extremely irritating.

Many elderly people who are slightly deaf turn the disability to advantage by pretending not to hear when it suits them. My Chap is convinced that dogs do the same. He might be right, in which case it is another feature which we share. I am sure we are bright enough to exploit the possibility when we are called away from a delightful scent and need to linger. But it could be just stubbornness, to which I reckon we are all entitled as we become senior citizens. Anyway, that is the line I will take when I am getting grey in the muzzle through all that worrying I do about the welfare of my couple. There has to be some reward!

7 Feeling My Way

. . . the exquisite touch, which renders ordinary commonplace things and characters interesting.

Having no hands and, in particular, no fingertips, my mouth is my main manipulator and also a major organ of touch – which is why I like to put things into it. Taking your hand into my mouth is also a show of affection – depending, of course, on how I do it! Considering my array of teeth and the potential strength of my jaws, I can be remarkably gentle, as I always want to be with those I love, though sometimes I may make a slight mistake in the rough and tumble of a game. My Chap's old springer spaniels had such 'soft' mouths that they could pick up an egg and carry it to him without a tooth mark on it. He tried to get me to do it but I knew about eggs in the past and immediately broke it so I could eat it – not one of his more successful experiments! Still, my mouth can be as gentle and soft as any spaniel's, as those who have ever given me a chocolate drop can testify.

I also do a lot of touching with my nose and lips – what my Chap calls a wuffle, a gesture which I reserve for the highly privileged. Wuffling, the softest of soft bites, is immensely important to me in keeping the bond between me and mine really tight.

Our tongues are sensitive to touch as well as taste and some dogs lick anybody they approve of, though I do it only on occasion when I need to show special affection or sympathy. We were doing it long before humans used their lips in greeting so perhaps we invented the kiss. Sometimes when I lick other things I am just giving them the stamp of ownership!

The outer part of my nose is also rich in touch cells with sensitive nerve endings and I use that on occasion to find out what kind of trousers the Chap is wearing – the walks kind or the London kind – by giving them a little prod with my snout. I can usually tell by smell and appearance but I like to make sure. Corduroys, which he never wears for London, are the easiest to detect by prod. And by smell, too, for that matter.

The array of long whiskers arising out of little bumps on the sides of my jowls and on my chin are particularly sensitive to touch. The Old Zoologist, who always likes to air his knowledge, calls them vibrissae – from the Latin for a nostril hair. I don't have any hairs in my nostrils but you do and, in men, they seem to get bigger as they get older, like their ears appear to. I don't know whether women's ears get bigger, because they continue to hide them with their hair.

Like your skin, mine is the largest organ of my body and is very sensitive to touch even though it is densely covered with hair. When we lived in packs we were very much contact animals in contrast to other creatures which cannot bear to be close, except when they are mating. So touch was very consoling to us as we slept together for protection and warmth. That is why we like being stroked and being close to you. However, like all creatures, including you, I react immediately to the slightest suspicious touch if I am caught unawares because, way back in our past, that could be a most dangerous position to be in.

My tail is specially sensitive to touch and, in that respect, is an important extension of my body, helping to warn me of sly attacks from behind and to take evasive action.

Our fur is also very sensitive to air currents ruffling it. A slight breeze is pleasant to us but I don't like a strong wind – especially when it blows up my tail! It is partly for that reason that I hate the flea-spray, though the smell and the cooling effect are also horrid. I am apt to get the flea-spray whenever I indulge in a really good scratch but the Chap often scratches and I never see him spraying himself.

The skin below my fur senses any change in temperature, which is a kind of touch because it is usually the effect of the air impinging on it. I don't shiver because my coat is so thick but other dogs with silky coats, like spaniels, do. All that their muscles are doing is trying to generate a little more body heat because they lose so much of it in a chill wind or in icy water. I do pant, however, if my skin or blood gets too warm, because that is the only way I can get rid of excess heat quickly. I may breathe at a rate of 300 pants a minute, or even 400, if I am very hot through exertion. It looks alarming but it is all perfectly normal. You would think you were dying if anything like that happened to you and you would probably be right.

For some time my couple wondered why I took a sudden dislike to being on their bed while they read the papers in the morning. I slid off back to my chair after only a few minutes. Then the penny dropped – with the colder weather they had started using the electric overblanket. I wasn't being huffy I was just too hot.

A dog's pads and its body in general are highly sensitive to vibrations from the earth and I make regular use of this ability when I am down by the canal or the river. I can sense the vibrations of the water voles moving in their burrows even before I can smell them. Sometimes

70

my Chap is amazed to see me run perhaps twenty yards and then point at something in the vegetation which he did not even know existed. It is the same with moles on the Common. I can sense them moving about below the ground and solved a mystery which has puzzled the Old Zoologist for years – where do all the moles go to in dry weather? Sometimes there are no molehills on the Common for weeks on end and as the mole has to eat worms continuously to stay alive he thought they must have migrated to damper places near the river. Not only did I prove to him that they are still active in their tunnels deep down below, by making it clear that I could sense them, but also convinced him that they hunt worms and other things on the surface in the matted grass, especially when dew brings the worms up. I caught one of these 'gentlemen in the velvet jacket' there and found several others. The Chap was very impressed and showed me one of the quite enormous fleas that live on all moles, many times bigger than a dog flea. I wouldn't like to be bitten by one of those. Poor mole!

I have never been in an earthquake but where these have occurred dogs have sensed them seconds before humans could detect a tremor.

I can also detect familiar bumps and turnings on the roads when I am in the car. I don't have to look up to know that I am nearing home or getting near the river when we go fishing. When we are going to a shoot, even a strange one, I know that when we are on the main roads there will be little to interest me and I curl up and sleep. But as soon as we turn into a lane I become excitedly alert and on the lookout for pheasants. When I enter the beautiful Hippenscombe Valley leading to the gun school where the Chap goes to practise and, hopefully, correct his faults, I know right away where I am. It is quite unconscious. A kind of feel memory, I suppose.

Like all highly developed creatures we dogs feel pain through special sense cells in the skin and joints and round our internal organs. It is a valuable danger signal inducing us to lick a sore place with antiseptic saliva and helps to tell us when something is wrong inside. We can bruise but not to the extent you do and it is not just because our fur protects us, though the fact that you are almost naked may have something to do with the hypersensitivity of your skin.

Like you, we sometimes give tongue with a yelp when we are hurt, there being no canine curses which you find so useful on such occasions. For instance, I always give an involuntary yelp when I happen to touch an electric sheepfence. Since most things have a purpose what is the use of the yelp? Well it lets you know that we are hurt and may need attention. So I suppose that in former days we yelped to let the rest of the pack know that we were hurt. It may be for the same reason that you give vent to expressions of pain. A solitary animal would not have much to gain by drawing attention to its pain. Indeed, it might induce predators to attack it. So I would not be surprised to learn that non-pack animals do not cry out when they are hurt, like you and I do.

It is clear to me, by comparing my behaviour with my Chap's, that we are nothing like as sensitive to pain as humans are. I can bump my head, shoulder or shin really hard on heavy furniture and hardly feel any discomfort, regularly amazing my Chap and disconcerting the Boss in this way. Considering how important my nose is to me it is, perhaps, surprising that it hurts so little when I stub it on something, like the dog-door when I don't know that it has been locked. Fortunately it is rubbery and, being where it is, it is the likeliest part of me to get knocked and I couldn't be yelping all the time. The tip of your nose also happens to be one of your least pain-sensitive spots. Isn't it amazing how alike we are?

I have never been badly bitten – yet – and being a female I don't suppose I ever will be, but I was badly kicked by a horse once and had to have stitches. After the initial fright I did not feel a lot of pain and fighting dogs seem to take little notice of really bad bites. According to doctors, the pain of human childbirth can be the worst, even when it is absolutely normal, but having pups hardly bothers us.

There seems to be a thing called the pain threshold – the level at which an unpleasant experience begins to be hurtful – and ours seems to be a lot higher than yours, for which, I think, we ought to be grateful. What dog in its right senses would want to feel pain?

Frankly, I think it is the human body that is at fault. It has something to do with the structure of your brain and your peculiar psychology, much pain being in the mind. It is a penalty for being able to think too deeply, if you like, for it is the part of your brain that gives you the intellectual edge over us where much of your pain is felt. Further, you are aware that certain kinds of pain may mean that there is something seriously wrong with you and that frightens you and may make the pain worse. Your power of imagination, from which we are virtually free, may intensify these effects. It also seems likely to me that you have all become too soft in the course of your evolution and civilization, a situation which, I suppose, also threatens us.

In addition, you suffer from much pain which we do not experience because your body is a makeshift. It was originally designed for walking on four legs, which is much more sensible in engineering terms, but was then converted to walking on two. As a result, your load-bearing is all wrong. All your weight is on two legs instead of on four so you get aches and pains in your back and joints. You suffer from slipped discs and your arches collapse. Your internal organs don't hang properly, so you get hernias. Your balance is precarious so you are prone to serious falls which break your bones and kill a lot of old people. And your females are inclined to have trouble, as well as pain, with childbirth.

Some dogs develop slipped discs and other spinal problems but they are the breeds, like the dachshund, which have been deliberately elongated by man to suit his weird fancies. I am grateful that I not only walk on four legs but am in the right proportions.

There seems to be a link between pain and pleasure. A tickle can go on for so long that it can become an unbearable pain (though I can't see that happening to me). It is the same with an itch which soon becomes unbearable but gives us both such pleasure when we can scratch it. Pleasant warmth can become extremely painful if it increases beyond a certain limit. So can a very loud noise. Could your sensitivity to pain therefore be linked somehow with the human addiction to pleasure? I leave it to you to decide.

No doubt, some people experience pain more severely than others, as may well be true of some dogs, but to judge by your poets, some of you seem to find the whole of life rather painful. Your problem seems to be finding a meaning to life – what is it all about? Thank Heaven (whatever that may be) that we are not burdened with such pointless questions. We just press on, confident that the best is yet to come.

8 Timing Isn't Everything

What is this life if, full of care,
Dogs have no time to stand and stare.

Like all creatures, save for those living totally in darkness, the rhythm of our lives used to be governed by the rotation of the earth on its axis, which is responsible for night and day. By nature, our biorhythm is quite different from yours. Yours is conditioned by the fact that you are active during the daylight and sleep during darkness. So you have a daily rhythm of feeling active during the day and feeling sleepy at night. Ours is different. We were conditioned by circumstances to be active at any time, day or night, so we have no fixed rhythm. Through habit, we tend to follow your pattern but we can still sleep any time and are always ready for action.

In the wild the seasons must have been very important to us, with winter being a tough time in the northern latitudes. But you have ironed all that out for us and except for gun dogs, who work mainly in the autumn and winter, all the months are more or less the same.

There can be no doubt that we have some kind of internal clock, which gives us a sense of time, though I do not know where it is. I know within a few minutes when it is time for my daily meal – around 4.00 p.m. in this household. For most of the day I have no interest in the burr of the electric can-opener but when I hear it in mid-afternoon I know it is for me and start jumping about.

One of my admirers sent the Chap a wall clock with a Labrador's head painted on it and he put it up in the study. I suppose it was a present for both of us but dogs don't need clocks, though they might occasionally be useful if fitted with alarms for feeding time and going-out time. I heard of a golden retriever which had been trained to serve as an alarm clock. Every morning it tapped at its Chap's bedroom door. The call was timed on four consecutive mornings at 7.22 a.m. precisely. Farm dogs will sometimes round up cows and bring them in to be milked at the right time on their own initiative but they may get some clues to the time from other activities on the farm, such as the readying of milk churns.

I know, again to within a few minutes, when it is time for my walks and I do not need any clues for that. In fact I usually go into the Chap's study about five minutes early to make sure he gets the message. I suspect that this time sense is something we acquired through you when you foisted the clock on us. In the wild we would have been governed by the light and by hunger pangs but would never have been dominated by time as you are. Your lives are run, literally, like clockwork, with your waking, meals, work periods and social engagements all at appointed times. It is no exaggeration to say that most of you are pathologically preoccupied with time. You rush about and speed in cars to 'save time', with which you often do little of much consequence. In the process you slaughter wildlife and dogs as well as yourselves. When you retire from business you are usually presented with a clock so that you can continue to be regulated by it.

As I have said, my Chap won't waste a minute and I can only describe him as an old man in a hurry. He works in his study until his wife bullies him out of it. He never sits in his garden unless he is correcting proofs. For any writer who has to earn his living, time is money but it is not just that. For him, time is the most precious commodity which must be put to maximum use – an idea which is crazy to me and to any other dog. It is a self-imposed rat race but most other men I encounter are equally obsessed by the clock and governed by it. Apart from feeding time, going-out time and lights out, time means little to me and I like it that way.

We do, however, share with you the experience that time drags on some occasions and goes like a flash on others. It drags when my Chap is held up from one of our walks by a long telephone call, and it races away when we're down on the river. The Chap insists that, for humans, time flies faster as they get older – it drags when they are school-children and gallops away when they are elderly. He doesn't understand why but there is a possible solution. When he was 10, a year was a big slice of time because it was only a tenth of all the life that he had experienced. When he got to 70, a year was a 70th of his total life so it was bound to appear to be shorter and to go faster – maybe seven times as fast. Further, a year is now a high proportion of what he has left and he is conscious of that.

I suppose we may experience the same phenomenon, though on a smaller scale because our lives are so much shorter, but except when there is some pleasure immediately in the offing, time means next to nothing to us. Perhaps one of the best services we give you is the calming effect of our relaxed presence, making you less conscious of time, at least for a while.

There is one aspect of time in which we greatly differ from you and of which you need to take continual note if you are going to treat us fairly. Our memory for most events is short and, usually, we soon forget not only something that happened but when it happened. So it is no good punishing us for something that occurred half an hour ago or even a few minutes ago. We won't associate the punishment with the offence so it will do no good and, in fact, we will be totally bewildered. Punishment under such circumstances can even be counter-productive, as the saying is. For example, if you chastise us for running away, when we finally return we will think we are being punished for coming back and will be less likely to do so next time.

Just as our memory for time past is usually short, so is our concept of the future. The next feeding time and walking time are the usual limits of the future in our minds. But this carries an advantage. We are free from long-term hope which plays such a part in your lives causing much human disappointment. We can be briefly disappointed, most commonly through broken promises, as when you assure us that we are going out and then change your minds. Promises to dogs should be kept.

There is another aspect of time which we share with you and all other creatures – our lifetime is finite and there comes a time to die. Fortunately, we are spared any awareness of the inevitability of death which is, uniquely, your predicament and another penalty you pay for your power of imagination. On average we are at a decided disadvantage regarding longevity. We should be grateful to you for giving us a substantially longer span of life than we could have expected in the wild, with all its hazards, especially during the puppy stage. But while a human female can expect a life of well over seventy years the best I can expect is about fourteen, though there are exceptions. Sadly, larger dogs have shorter life spans, the records being held by little dogs like fox terriers. It must be the sheer wear and tear of carrying so much weight around that gives giant dogs like wolfhounds and mastiffs such a short allotted time. It seems to be the same with the human species. It is the little ones that generally last longest. I am told that intermittent starvation can extend life span but I do not think I will be trying it. Neither will the Chap.

As with humans some of us age more rapidly than others and show it, but our predicament is so much better than yours. By and large we do not show our age like you do, with all your wrinkles, blotchy skin, bent backs and baldness, and we generally grow old more gracefully. Fortunately there is no evidence that dogs come to look like their Chaps, which is just as well because bald or half-bald dogs would look very odd, though only because, in contrast to human baldies, you are not used to seeing them. We are not really aware of the ageing process, as some women are, so painfully. We live for the day, taking time as it ticks, and I propose to go on enjoying every minute of it.

9 Intelligence – A Matter of Definition

*It is not the insurrections of ignorance that are
dangerous but the revolts of intelligence.*

Scientists have spent a long time arguing about whether
dogs are intelligent or not. In their vanity, some of
them claim that intelligence is restricted to the human
species and its monkey relatives by defining it in a
highly specialized way. They say that intelligence is
the capacity to deal with a novel situation by novel
means. In tests comparing this capacity in monkeys
and dogs they assessed the ability of both to find
their way out of big puzzle boxes fitted with various
latched doors and other obstacles. The monkeys did
much better than we did. In fact we were judged as
doing so badly that we failed. So what? When am I
going to need to find my way out of puzzle boxes?
Instead of wasting time looking for latches I would
simply go on barking until somebody came to let me
out. Hardly less intelligent than the idiot who put me
in the box in the first place!

In fact, come to think of it, I can find my way out
of the only puzzle box that is likely to confront me.
The two dog-flap doors which lead in and out of
the kitchen and conservatory to the garden consti-
tute a puzzle box. How long did it take me to learn
them, once they had been pointed out to me? Like

ten minutes! I'll bet I could find my way out of the Hampton Court maze quicker than most humans because I would simply follow the scent of the people who have already made their way out by trial and error. Nothing unintelligent about that!

Maybe the scientists used the wrong dogs in their experiments. For something like forty years my Chap used short leads attached to a metal spike stuck in the ground to keep his springer spaniel gun dogs tethered when he was shooting. He tried it with me and I simply dug the spike out. Oddly, he was not annoyed, only immensely impressed with my brightness. I can't think why. The solution seemed obvious to me – it's common dog-sense that what goes straight in must come straight out, if the ground is soft enough to excavate. I only wonder why none of the spaniels had ever thought of it. It must be that some breeds – and some individual dogs, especially bitches – are brighter than others. When I continued to dig or pull the straight spike out he threatened me with a spike like a giant corkscrew which was invented for tethering goats. To my mind, though, there are not many things that are beyond the wit of dog. I reckon that what screws in must also screw out. If that fails, I could always get the lead into such a mess round the corkscrew that he would have to release me.

Without being told, I know that I have to be gentle with children and take a lot more pulling about from them than I would from an adult. I am also specially careful when I take their hands in my mouth.

The moment I see the Chap filling his briefcase I know that he is going to London and that I must concentrate my attention on the Boss to take me out. Conversely, when he reaches for the shoehorn he keeps in his study I know we are going for a walk, as I also do when I see him switch on the answerphone. Without being taught to do it, my yellow Labrador friend, Burro, picks up a large tin bowl and carries it into the great hall of her house, keeping it in her mouth when tea and crumpets are served there after a shoot. She says nothing but buttery offerings pour in because guests find the spectacle irresistible – as she knows they will. How's that for initiative? According to the gentleman who bred me, my mother, Tarka, is even more astute. She can sort out four different bowls, and pick them up one by one in descending order of size, carrying each around until somebody puts something in one of them. It seems that, like a human trader, she starts with high hopes then gradually lessens her demands. So there is no shortage of acumen on that side of my family. I have heard of one dog which feigned lameness when faced with having work to do but was seen larking about normally with other dogs when it thought its master's back was turned. How's that for intelligence?

When my couple have guests to dinner I am shut in the Chap's study but if he comes and lets me out any time after 11.00 p.m. I know exactly what is expected of me. I rush into the living room and give him the chance to explain that I am creating a fuss because I need to be taken out which, of course, is rightly interpreted by the guests as a signal for them to leave. And that is only one of several social services I render.

Could we have survived all these years, especially in such close contact with the ruthless human species, if we had not been intelligent? Even by the scientists' definition, we have certainly shown outstanding ability to meet new situations quickly and successfully in our relationship with you. Once, when I was mooching through a wood, I was caught in a wire snare that had been set up by a gamekeeper to catch a fox. I had never faced that situation before so what did I do? Panic and pull the wire tighter as foxes often do until they are strangled? No way! I just sat still and barked until the Chap came and released me. The fox may be noted for cunning but I reckon I was a good deal wiser. I am not that short on cunning either. The Chap avoided prosecution by the Government so successfully when he was a newshound in Fleet Street that he became known as the Artful Dodger and I suppose I have learned a few things from him.

The simple truth – and that is all that matters – is that I am intelligent enough for my needs. Our intelligence is of a different order and the things we are not intelligent about don't matter to us. We are not four-legged humans in a fur coat, nor are we monkeys.

Let me give you my definition of intelligence, which should apply to the body as a whole, not just to the brain. It is the ability to cope effectively with any situation I am likely to face in every-day life. I can do that fine, being very much a dog of the world, even if I am only three years old. As the Chap says, I am a prodigy in more ways than one.

At this point let me debunk the old wives' tale that one year in a dog's life corresponds to seven human years so that, at three, I should be compared with a girl of twenty-one. You may live seven times longer than we do, on average, but we mature much more rapidly. A dog is mentally mature by the time it is one year old, though it still has much to learn. I reckon that, at three, I represent a woman of at least forty so far as wiles are concerned.

As I have stressed in previous chapters, there are so many things which dogs can do that you can't. Some have demonstrated extraordinary ability to find their way home when they have been lost many miles away in countryside which they have never seen before – what humans now call orienteering. That situation would defeat most people if they had to do it without any help or without a compass or a map. There is one record of a red setter which had been taken more than twenty miles away from home to have a litter of pups. Having produced five she quickly disappeared with the pups and, many days later, turned up at her old home, emaciated but with all the pups in good condition. She must have walked hundreds of miles in carrying the pups one by one and must also have swum a wide river nine times, taking one pup in her mouth each time. Sustained effort on such a scale so soon after giving birth would have been beyond the physical power of any human mother.

All dogs have a rough sense of direction so that if we begin to try to find our way home at least we are not likely to go the wrong way. Then we cast about for some landmark we can recognize. If dogs are allowed to observe the route of a car journey by looking out of a window they can sometimes remember enough features to find their way back, but if they are in a closed container or simply not looking they are likely to fail, which is one reason why there are so many poor strays.

I don't know how well I would perform, myself, and I don't want to try but one of the Chap's shooting friends probably owes his life to the canine capability to sense direction. When he was young he was out wildfowling on some marshes with three men when fog came down. As the tide began to flow in they were totally lost in a maze of muddy creeks. The men had a springer spaniel with them and the master shouted, 'Go Home! Go Home!' The dog immediately knew the direction to take and the men followed it to safety. It is easy to dismiss such a feat as purely a homing instinct but that doesn't explain it, does it? Instinct is supposed to be an inborn facility to react to a stimulus in a certain way without conscious thought, and we are assuredly stronger on it than you are, but there is growing evidence that much animal behaviour that has been airily dismissed as 'instinctive' is really the result of experience. Take swimming for instance. What do we or any other four-legged animals do when we get out of our depth in water for the first time? We just keep on walking or running, making the same leg motions as we would on land. In our horizontal position our natural buoyancy keeps us afloat and the legs keep us moving forwards. We would only be surprised if they didn't. Your position is different because your vertical stance gives you inadequate buoyancy. If you lie on your stomach and 'dog paddle' you don't sink. You need to be taught to swim as well as we can because just walking in the water won't do the trick, but once we have learned to walk on land – by trial and error as you do – we automatically know how to swim. So does a horse, a cow, a rabbit, even a pig. There is really nothing 'instinctive' about it. A puppy which has not yet learned to walk will drown.

Many other things that we animals do are not completely inborn, as once thought, but are taught to us by our mothers and by the pack, just as happens with human babies. Some reasoning power is involved and it must be obvious to all that we learn the necessary behaviour much more quickly than any human infant. So our brains and nervous systems would seem to be quicker on the uptake than yours.

Scientists have put a lot of effort into comparing the brains of dogs and men. The human brain is, admittedly, more complex and capable of greater ingenuity but that only makes it more unfair to compare our two intelligences. You should only compare like with like and our intelligence is of a different kind. Further, you should not restrict the comparison to the brain, in my view. It is fashionable to compare the brain to a computer but it is the whole body which acts like a computer, not just the brain, and that is especially true of the dog. So you need to compare the reactions of our whole bodies to situations and in many of them we score.

Nobody who has watched a gun dog, a guide dog or, indeed, kept any kind of dog, can doubt that we have outstanding ability to learn. A guide dog can even be trained to warn his blind owner to avoid overhead obstacles, like wires. When you think of the time, effort and money put into human education – and with such modest results – compared with that devoted to teaching dogs, I think we do remarkably well. Scientists try to explain away the skills we learn by saying that the canine brain builds up a store of conditioned reflexes – automatic reactions – to what we should do and should not do. But you do exactly the same, in learning to drive a motorcar, for instance, and you count that as being intelligent. In fact, conditioned reflex experiments have shown that our two species are very alike in this respect. For example, we both learn to limit our naturally aggressive behaviour, though I think we succeed better than many of you do individually and certainly better than you do as a species. We do not commit genocide.

I have learned to know when I have done something likely to bring admonishment, which is another way of saying that I understand guilt. This is quite an intellectual feat because I have not done anything wrong by canine standards, only by the Chap's view of how I should behave. As most Chaps and Bosses know, a dog has a guilty look when it knows it has taken a chance and is likely to make itself scarce, as I do at such unfortunate times by hiding behind the big fuel tank in the back of the garden.

Being able to remember is another essential aspect of intelligence and, though our memory is inferior to yours in some ways, in others it is superior, such as our recollection of smells, some sounds and locations. We can retain scent pictures in our memories which you cannot begin to grasp. Of course the power of memory varies from dog to dog, like yours does, but mine seems to be pretty good. There have been many occasions when I have had to jog the Boss's memory, about feeding me, for instance, especially when she has been talking on the telephone.

We also exhibit curiosity, which is an essential component of intelligence. I am intensely inquisitive about everything, especially about anything new that comes into the house, such as a piece of furniture, a carpet, a cushion, a coat or even a new ornamental jug. I have to keep a mental inventory of all my property, don't I? A few things continue to fascinate me even when I am used to them. When the Chap winds up the grandfather clock I am always intrigued by those huge weights that make it work.

Speech is supposed to be one of the highest expressions of human intelligence and, though we do not speak as you do, we can communicate very effectively both with our own kind and with you. We do have quite a complicated language, as I shall prove in the next chapter. And we can learn quite a lot of your language, verbs as well as nouns.

We also have understanding in the sense of being able to discern situations, appreciating their significance and giving comfort to those affected. I can tell by the tone of my Chap's voice, by changes in his scent, even by his posture – that hang-man look – when he is frustrated or unhappy and I do my best to comfort him. It is no fluke that I happen to put my snout on his lap and look at him with adoring eyes when he is distressed. The Boss was very touched when I licked the bandage on her finger which she had cut while opening a tin. Some cynics might think that I just liked the taste of the bandage but wounded flesh gives off a peculiar scent and wolves of the same pack lick each others' wounds. Licking keeps a wound clean and our saliva has antiseptic qualities. So I was using my intelligence as well as showing sympathy.

Many humans might not do too well under my definition of intelligence – the ability to cope effectively with any situation you are likely to face in every-day life. As I have been at some pains to point out, mass human behaviour does not seem very intelligent by our standards and many people make an unholy mess of their private lives, bringing unhappiness on themselves, their families and their dogs, which usually suffer when there is a break-up. This applies even to those judged to be among the most intelligent – your philosophers, like Bertrand Russell, who hardly set a sensible example in their own lives. That fellow, Socrates, even took his own life, something a dog would never do.

In short, to us, much of human life looks more like a tale told by an idiot than intelligent behaviour. As I have observed, there is a profound difference between knowledge and wisdom, which is the ability to make sensible use of knowledge. The first should lead to the second but it rarely seems to in the human world. According to an old Irish saying, 'There came an old prophecy out of a bog that Ireland be ruled by an ass and a dog.' We could not have made a worse job of it!

I seriously suspect that there are more wise dogs than wise people. Take the Chap, for instance. He is forever urging economy but never knows how much money is in his wallet and never counts his change, assuming that everyone is honest and infallible when he knows that some are neither. Let him loose in a supermarket or cash-and-carry and there's no holding him. He sweats his guts out to write an article for a couple of hundred pounds but pays scant attention to his investments which could make him far more with less effort. He would rather spend three hours writing than three minutes to fill in a form. He puts off going to the doctor but would rush me to the vet at the first sign of sickness. Hardly wise behaviour and maybe not even intelligent. But he is not exceptional.

Most of you, at some stage in your lives, have an irrational fear of the dark which is just another part of the day to us. So many of you have phobias which to us are laughable. The Boss is so allergic to snakes that she has to cover her eyes if one appears on television, yet it is only a harmless picture. The Chap is equally allergic to pop music and goes mad if a car parks outside his study window with the car radio blaring away. To me it's just another harmless noise.

You set such store by education yet your children continue to make all the mistakes you and your parents made. This includes dependence on alcohol and even more injurious drugs. You are born with a body and brain which develop into a marvellous machine yet, from an early age, you begin to damage it, deliberately. Neither we nor any other creature has ever been guilty of such stupidity.

You behave as though the planet existed just for you. 'What use are these creatures?' you ask. If the answer seems negative you destroy them, calling them vermin.

If a dog appears with inheritable features which are clearly bad then the human breeders make sure it is not allowed to reproduce. When humans are born with such faults they are not only permitted to breed but are encouraged by do-gooders to do so. This may seem humane for those individuals but not for their children, who are going to inherit the same disabilities, nor for the human species as a whole.

I have heard a highly successful friend of my Chap say that 80 per cent of humans never think and that the other 20 per cent should be grateful because they can take advantage of it. Could anything be more cynical?

Though 'cynical' means 'dog-like' (because another Greek philosopher, Diogenes, was stupid enough to live in a tub like a dog), we would never be so beastly to another of our own kind who did not happen to be bright. Dog does not exploit dog but man exploits man all the time.

There are many of you who seem to be keen to be exploited. Take much of modern art, for instance. Three lines scrawled on a canvas and they bring more than a million pounds at a sale! I could create as good a picture with a brush tied to my tail. Perhaps I should try and found a new art form – Didoism. The Chap is sure that some idiot critic might well declare it to be great art, full of poignant significance, which the taxpayers should acquire for the nation, if he did not know it was the work of a dog.

Further, it is the so-called intelligent – the 20 per cent – who are responsible for the development of weapons of mass destruction and for all the damage to the environment through development, industry, 'scientific' farming, and pollution. Dogs never learned to use tools like you did but look what you have done with them! Compared with man's inhumanity to man, dog's incaninity to dog is as nothing.

Many revolutionaries were thought to be so intelligent as to be called intellectuals, and look at the misery and suffering they inflicted on the world in trying to enforce their crackpot theories on 'the masses'. In that connection some of the experiments carried out on dogs have shown a further similarity with the human species. Just as every man has his breaking point, so has every dog. We can both be brainwashed.

Either the human race is too intelligent for its own good or, by my definition, its intelligence is limited because while it is able to cope with most of the situations which Nature presents it is unable to cope with those it creates itself. One thing is certain – while

I am no intellectual, I am intelligent enough to get my way and without having to do much work for it. Perhaps it is in my interest that my intelligence should be underestimated. Otherwise my Chap would expect too much of me.

One unfortunate consequence of being intelligent is mental disorder because when a brain is so complex something is bound to go wrong with it at times, either before birth or later in life. We therefore have our share of individuals who are mentally handicapped or mentally unbalanced. Nobody has yet devised an accurate way of measuring the Intelligence Quotients of dogs but it is self-evident that, since their brains vary so much, there will be some with higher than average IQs while a few will be stupid. What you get when you buy a young puppy is largely a matter of luck.

As an example of mental instability, vets recognize a condition called the 'rage syndrome' when a dog, usually male, has the habit of flying into a raging tantrum. It is supposed to be inherited but, whatever the cause, I reckon that it is commoner in human males.

Few can doubt that there is a far greater proportion of mad humans than mad dogs but that is only to be expected when the human brain is so much more complex and, therefore, more likely to go wrong. What surprises me is that irrational storms do not happen more often!

There is a recognized form of human madness, called cynanthropy, in which a person fancies he is changed into a dog and imitates its habits, barking compulsively, among other things. I suppose that, to some extent, most of us are touched with the reverse – anthrocyny – but not compulsively, only to the extent that suits us.

Becoming semi-human, as so many of us are, is supposed to lay a dog open to human psychological trouble like complexes and neuroses. I wonder what I have got and what use I can make of it. I don't think

I have any psychological kinks – yet – but, then, those so afflicted rarely realize that they are. My Chap thinks I'm kinky when I roll in cow dung on the Common and I have to admit I don't know why I do it. At least, I don't eat it as some dogs do. I enjoy being washed after it, especially if he uses the hosepipe but, frankly, I don't really think that far ahead. Maybe it's a hangover from wolf days. I wonder if wolves rolled in caribou dung to disguise their scent when they were creeping up on the caribou? If they did I could claim that the habit is not crazy but part of my 'culture' and, in the current climate, that should entitle me to do it, however anti-social it might be.

I suppose that some dogs suffer from depression, which could account for their hang-dog look but I never get depressed except in the small degree when I can see that the Chap is going out and not taking me. I quickly get over it because a dog needs to treat any situation as it is and not as it ought to be.

There is at least one fully documented account of a canine Oedipus complex in an eight-year-old male golden retriever. Its entire life had been spent with its mother and, though larger, was very submissive to her. Efforts to make him breed were made but he would never show any interest in any other bitch.

To nobody's surprise, perhaps, there are canine psychiatrists in America treating dogs for their insecurity complexes, inferiority feelings, anxiety neuroses and even kleptomania, some dogs being unable to resist stealing food. I wonder what the canine couch looks like and whether the patient is made to lie on it. The Chap once knew a psychiatrist in London who was called in to treat a famous racehorse called Aureole, belonging to the Queen. Aureole's problem was being difficult at the start of a race so the psychiatrist needed to convince the horse that this was a bad thing. All he did was to stand for several long sessions with his index finger in the horse's anus. He claimed that this put him *en rapport* with the animal and enabled him to pass soothing advice to it. The treatment seemed to work but I hope I am never subjected to it. A thermometer in that place, when the vet takes my temperature, is bad enough.

I suppose the commonest behavioural complaint about a dog is that it is 'spoiled' by being over-humanized. But what does it mean? Spoiled for any form of work? What does that matter if you are not going to do any? I suppose it means over-indulged and paid too much attention. But there is nothing wrong with that so long as both sides enjoy it and a dog is not overfed. And what about people being 'spoiled' by dogs? We never hear complaints about that yet the extent of our affection and dutiful submission is so great as to be grossly flattering. Does that impair the human character? If it does, then millions of you are 'spoiled' beyond redemption. My Chap has been heavily caninized by fawning attention for over forty years. I suppose it must have exerted some effect on his character. (By the way, I don't think that he runs any risk of being canonized!)

OK, I'm spoiled if you insist – but isn't it lovely? And think of all those poor dogs which aren't.

10 Canine Communications

Give every dog thine ear

Humans have described dogs and every other non-human species as 'dumb animals' but I don't think any animals are really dumb, dogs least of all. Not only do we have a language based on noises which come out of our mouths but we can communicate, both dog-to-dog and dog-to-man, in many other different ways by body language. Instant communication was essential in a pack on the hunt, when the situation was changing every moment as the prey tried to defeat our game plan for bringing it down. We still retain that capability and much more besides. The degree of communication between dog and man is far more definite than with any other creature. Just watch a sheepdog trial, a gun dog working to orders in the heather or a guide dog conducting its sightless charge through city streets. As for being a dumb brunette, in that other sense of the word – well ask the Chap.

When you think of communication it is speech that comes to mind, gestures and other forms of body language being auxiliary. With us it is the reverse. Communication by sound, of which we can make a great variety, has always been essential to creatures with a complex social life but I will first explain our more basic means of making our wants and meaning felt.

I have already dealt with our scent communications with other dogs and with humans and will just remind you that when a dog leaves his scent mark he is communicating with all other dogs as certainly as a man who puts up a message on a poster. When dog meets dog one of the first things they do is to sniff each other and since this is mutual it is a form of communication – a sizing-up and look-see ritual, as when two people shake hands. We concentrate first on the rear end which tells us quite a lot. It wouldn't do for you. In fact it would probably get you locked up. But our approach is more hygienic because, though we get close to sniff, we don't touch. We remain literally a whisker away. When you shake hands you do touch, very firmly, and one of my Chap's doctor friends is convinced that a lot of colds are transmitted that way. So much so that he won't shake hands with anyone who's got a cold. As for kissing, of which you do such a lot socially, there is no doubt about that being a major means for the transmission of germs. We also do quite a lot of sniffing round the mouth but we don't actually touch there either. As I have said, we do a certain amount of licking as a special mark of affection, both towards dogs and humans, but rarely mouth to mouth with other dogs.

Through smell and other clues I can detect changes of moods in other dogs and appreciate their significance. This was important in the pack to sense any hostility from other members and, especially, to know whether the leader was angry or in an aggressive mood. The smell of bad temper, in either a dog or a human, is both sudden and strong. A female dog is never in much danger of being bitten by a male. All male dogs may be sons of bitches but there are no battered wives in dogdom, such violent displays of cowardice being restricted to your world. But it is particularly important to the male that he should not lose face in front of a bitch, as I believe it is in the human sphere. So in our pack era we always did what we could to avoid trouble, as I do to this day in conformity with my instincts. If I sense that the Chap or the Boss is ill-tempered I disappear until the mood has changed. That makes for peace all round. So the old manners of the canine world still hold good. They were all unwritten but, by and large, they were obeyed and saved an awful lot of hassle and unnecessary wounds which could always be dangerous in the wild, where there were no vets to stitch them up or sterilize them. It would be fair to say that, regarding the social need to behave to a required standard, doggers maketh dog. Another way we resemble each other!

Like most females, I can communicate with my eyes to some degree. Watching a dog's or a human's eyes can tell us both a great deal. I avert my gaze, as humans do, when I feel guilty over something I have done. My eyes have tear glands to keep them moist but I cannot weep to communicate my sorrow or to extract sympathy and make a man feel guilty, as women do, so expertly. (To test my tear glands the Chap tried peeling a pickling onion in front of my nose but one whiff of that alien vapour was enough for me. In the ensuing battle of wills he was the only one who ended in tears. It seems to me that if man is really clever he would have developed a vegetable which makes him laugh.)

Sometimes the Boss says I even look soulful, though dogs are not supposed to have souls. I suppose that my eyes contribute something to my smile, though this is more of a general facial expression. When I smile – and I do a lot of it – my lips are slightly curled to expose the tips of what the Chap calls my Dracula teeth – my canines. Its message is clear and straightforward – 'I like what you are doing. Please carry on doing it.' My smile is always honest, as are the rest of my communications. With you, a smile, and even what you say, often covers what you are really thinking.

The degree to which I bare my teeth speaks volumes, both to other dogs and to humans. A modest baring can be a welcome but there can be no doubting what a major exposure means, especially if accompanied by a snarl, for we always give warning that you are making things dangerous for yourself, if you are sharp enough to interpret it. You don't use your teeth much in this way but you might reveal your feelings by gritting them.

We can also use our teeth in a negative way for communicating. I can mouth a little girl's hand so affectionately that she will not feel my teeth. Or I can give the Boss a nip with my incisors, so delicate that she knows it is an expression of fun. We have the equipment to inflict terrible wounds if we were driven to it but that is not the nature of my breed, even if cruelly treated. Occasionally a normally docile dog will bite its master, quite savagely, spaniels, even females, being notorious in that respect. Nobody knows what they are communicating when they do it. Sometimes, perhaps, it represents years of pent-up dislike – the 'she was his dog and he done her wrong' syndrome. More likely, though, it is the result of an unaccountable brainstorm.

Our range of facial expressions, which is much wider than anyone who is not a dog can appreciate, was inherited from wolves, who still use them a lot. Apart from looking happy, hopeful, doleful, dejected and disappointed I can look what the Boss calls 'brassed off' when the couple both insist on reading the newspapers when I would like them to attend to me.

Sadly, some types of dog, like the poor Old English sheepdog, have been bred to have so much hair on their faces that they cannot make full use of facial expressions. I wonder if men who grow great hairy beards and moustaches do so to hide their true feelings, like women used to wear veils to make themselves more inscrutable.

With dog-to-man communication it does not help that we are always communicating upwards. While you regard staring as ill-mannered we do a lot of it at you and at other dogs, the length and nature of the stare being full of meaning. It tends to be accompanied by variations in the position and stance of the body, posture being an important way of communicating between dogs. The attitude of the body, and especially the head, ears and tail, speaks volumes, especially if accompanied by a bristling of the hackles and the fur in general. A dog on the verge of attacking makes itself look as big as possible to overawe its opponent while a submissive dog crouches, legs bent and tail down, to look small.

One man soon knows what another means if he puts his fists up, or only two of his fingers, and dogs have an even greater range of communicating purely by motions. The whole gait of a dog can be very revealing, not only of intent, but general character. We can all tell the open-hearted dog, which I hope I am, and the slinking dog which is not to be trusted. I know, immediately, from the way a dog runs towards me whether it is friendly or not and it will rarely pretend to be friendly as a ruse to get close and then turn on me. Treachery of that sort is a human trait. Incidentally, when people go to buy a pup from a litter they often choose the one that runs towards them first but that one may be the most aggressive.

We have, of course, adapted our posture communications to life with you. The way I approach my Chap when it is time for a walk, or when I want to go further when he would like to return, is so eloquent as to be unmistakeable. Similarly, I recognize the significance of the Chap's posture when he shows me the dog lead. If my jealousy is aroused because the Boss is making a fuss of the Chap there can be no doubt what my reaction means – 'Would you mind putting my Chap down?' Likewise my expectant posture when I remind the Boss that it is feeding time is equally meaningful.

When I rush around and then stop and bow the front part of my body I am indicating that I am in the mood for play, especially if I have a ball or rubber bone in my mouth. Play was an important means of communication in our pack days and still is with puppies, who learn the means of communication that way. It also helps to keep older dogs young in heart. Toys are fun to play with on your own but not for long. Just as children need companionship during play so do we. That way we learn more from each other, and, of course, the basis of learning is communication.

I can also command attention for play by repeatedly pushing a ball or a stick at somebody so that they cannot avoid taking notice. This usually does the trick but I have had no co-operation on the occasions when I have done it with a small log from the garage woodpile while the Chap was bending down in the garden.

Sometimes I roll on my back and kick my legs in the air, time and again, to express my joy of living. If I do it while people are around I am communicating my happiness to them. If I happen to be on my own, as I often am when rolling on the lawn, then I am just telling the world in general that all is well with my bit of it and that it is great to be alive.

Another way in which we use our whole body to communicate our pleasure is to rub ourselves against the legs of those we love. I do admit, however, that I sometimes abuse this gesture when I am wet. The Chap's trousers are excellent for drying my face and coat, though he soon cottons on to what I am doing and I get what he calls 'the bum's rush'.

When I am particularly pleased to see anyone I waggle the whole of my body – what my Chap calls my Marilyn Monroe act. It is a motion in which the tail really does end up wagging the dog.

To most of you my tail is just something to wag but it is far more than that. It is my semaphore and a major part of my communicating system – something else I inherited from wolves who use their tails to express their moods. Like people gesture with their hands and arms – even when they are on the telephone and there's nobody to see them – I gesture with my tail in ways which are linked to the expressions on my face. I signal my peaceful intentions – or otherwise. When I sidle up with my tail stiffly erect and waving slowly from side to side I am matching for a fight. Rapid tail wagging from side to side is another counterpart of the human smile. I laugh with my tail and use it a lot because I have much to laugh about. Tail wagging also flings around the scent from my anal glands. Such is the versatility of its complex muscles that I can even give just the tip of it a gentle wag to welcome someone who enters a room while I am curled up resting, so that I don't have to bother to open my eyes. When I put my tail between my legs I am signalling submission – discretion usually being the better part of canine valour. I can also use my tail for protecting my assets when a dog, like my lecherous Labrador friend, Caesar Sieff, pays me unwanted attention. The whole poise of the canine tail says so much.

Just as some people gesture more than others, so do some dogs. My tail is certainly more waggish than most. I wonder if Italian dogs gesture in this way more than other dogs, through copying the habits of their masters and mistresses. Perhaps the Chap will make a study next time he is in Italy.

My tail is also useful to me when I am frustrated because then I can chase it round and round. I don't know why this 'displacement behaviour', as the scientists call it, helps but it does. I suppose it's the canine counterpart of the way the Chap bangs doors, curses and stomps about when he's annoyed or been thwarted.

By raising my tail I can make myself look bigger if I wish to impress, and by putting it between my legs make myself smaller if I wish to show submission.

I use my tail, perhaps inadvertently, to announce my arrival upstairs in the morning. It clonks on the radiator as I pass it in the corridor leading to the bedroom. On occasion, however, it gets me into trouble by sweeping the odd ornament off low tables and there was once a near-disaster. The Chap had bought one of those antique screens decorated with beautiful Victorian scraps and was repairing it in one of the bedrooms. I wandered in to greet him and my wagging tail bashed a hole in it. He was not best pleased but accepted that it was his fault for leaving the door open.

On the whole, though, I have to count myself very lucky to belong to a breed in which the tails are not docked. I feel sad for any dog that does not have a whole tail. Removing it virtually makes a dog half dumb. Sure, it can wag its stump but it can't signal properly and can't smile properly, and what a tragedy that is. I wonder if tailless dogs get the odd bite because they cannot signal submission quickly enough. Seriously, I doubt that a dog without a tail would last long in the wild.

Happily, it has now become illegal to remove any part of a dog's tail for any reason except when a qualified vet advises that it is in a dog's medical interest. Further, only a vet may do it while, in the past, puppy dogs' tails were even bitten off by country folk. So good riddance, I say, to what was a barbaric practice to satisfy the whims of show-dog people who even clipped boxers' ears for so-called cosmetic purposes.

Babies are sometimes born with a tail but the doctors always dock them completely. I suppose it shows that you once had a tail, way back in time, and are now ashamed of it. A pity, really. It would be most interesting for a dog to observe what you could do with it. Would you get your tail up when confident and have it between your legs when you are frightened or down in the dumps? The possibilities are enchanting.

Our general behaviour can also be a form of communication. Sometimes, when I run I do so in such a way that I am telling the Chap that I want him to run with me. Or I might bring him the lead or even my water bowl to have it filled. There was a case recently of a boxer dog which sought out her mistress's lipstick, after watching her at her make-up mirror, and daubed her own face up with it. An animal psychologist concluded that the dog was deliberately trying to show her mistress how close she was to her by mimicking what she did so that she could look like her. Of course, it could be that she liked the smell of the lipstick and licked it on to her face but it could have been a form of communication.

As to the question of our spoken language, which I call Doggish, scientists argued for many years that we do not really have one but behaviour experiments have now forced them to admit that they were wrong. They even discovered that bees communicate quite complex messages to each other by dancing around in various ways and several books have been published about the language of the bees. Well, if bees have a language we certainly do and we express it far more eloquently.

While your larynx and vocal cords give you a wider range of sounds, ours are versatile enough to produce at least thirty different meaningful noises, according to scientists who have listed them. Barking, of course, is our main form of audible expression and, for a female, I am well endowed in that respect. As in the human species, the males usually have deeper voices but I happen to have what the poet Byron called 'the watchdog's honest bark' and I am so pleased that I do not have a yap, as are those around me. Barking seems to be another thing we have picked up from you because wild wolves rarely bark though they learn to do so in captivity. Perhaps it was our attempt to mimic your speech and, over the centuries, man kept on selecting the best barkers for breeding because they were the most effective guard dogs. Anyway, I have different barks for different situations and I reserve the loudest and most savage-sounding for other dogs, especially those going past the house and whose paws I can just see under the double garden doors. It's not that I don't like other dogs. I do but my instincts tell me that I must let them all know that the territory is occupied and that it is never safe to let up on that precaution. My message is more 'be aware' of the dog rather than 'beware' of it. The neighbours are pretty understanding because I don't bark much at night, when there are no dogs passing anyway. It seems to be accepted round here that every dog is entitled to her woof and there is a spin off for them. I am part of the neighbourhood watch against vandals and intruders.

Of course I sometimes bark to draw human attention to myself. I might do it if I happen to have been shut out in the garden too long with the dog-door locked or shut up in the car when there are visitors who don't like dogs much. I might also bark a little through excitement.

When I hunt I do it silently because I can see no point in letting the target know that I am coming. Some breeds yelp as they hunt – the huntsmen call it 'music' – but silence seems more sensible and, contrary to fable, wolves hunt noiselessly. I am, of course, silent for most of my time and my couple and I are happy in each others' silences – until I get bored.

Just as every human has a recognizable voice, so dogs have distinctive barks which they can distinguish from a distance and that was important in keeping the pack together. As with human voices the range is infinite but we can still pick out those of known friends – and enemies. I have never heard of a stammering dog but it would be quite an interesting bark wouldn't it?

I do a daily stint of barking through the front door to let people know that there is a dog permanently on guard, which is also advertised by a notice on the gate, but occasionally the Chap gets sick of it and bawls me out for it. Eventually he solves the problem by taking me out to run off my energy. 'That dog's in a very barky humour,' he explains to the Boss as we set off. Another mission cleverly accomplished!

Both he and the Boss get very cross if I happen to bark during their post-lunch siesta and I have learned that it is wise to let sleeping men (and women) lie. So now I take a brief siesta myself, putting myself to bed, without being asked, as soon as lunch is over.

It is tough to be told off for a few woofs when humans never stop talking, especially as we communicate only when we need to while 90 per cent of what you utter is pointless wind. But what really irritates me is when I am told to stop barking because there is nothing there when I know that there is. It's odd how they forget that I can hear so many things they can't and it gives me great pleasure when I am proved right and that little tap on the front door turns into a sharp knock!

Like all dogs I can also growl, when I am suspicious, getting angry, or otherwise displeased, as I am with the odd villager, for reasons only I understand, but I do not do much of it. In the wild a sudden growl or grunt is usually an alarm signal among pack animals, indicating that danger threatens and fight, or flight, may be necessary. Gestures then spread the alarm through the pack which, of course, is always more alert than a single animal, like me. Still, I seem to do pretty well and since, in my case, flight is never necessary when I am inside my territory, my growl is smartly followed by a warning bark. I don't suppose that the bark really frightens other dogs, though. They know that there is truth in the old adage that it is the slowest barker that is the surest biter.

My grunts, apart from any which I may make in my sleep, are always unmistakeable expressions of deep contentment.

I do not howl much because I am hardly ever lonely but I often let one rip if my Chap gets out of sight on the river when I am pegged down. A dog has to express her displeasure sometimes. Wild dogs and wolves often howl together, perhaps to let other packs know where they are so that they can keep out of each others' way. It is not impossible that they simply enjoy it, like humans sing together for the pleasure of it, and, in both cases, community noise helps to bind social ties. Maybe dogs and wolves that howl together stay together.

There are stories of dogs howling at the moment when their masters died, as though there was some telepathy between them. Perhaps the most remarkable case was described to the Chap by the late Lord Carnarvon whose father was involved in the discovery of Tutankhamen's tomb. His father died from pneumonia in Cairo at five minutes to two on the morning of 5 April 1923 and, at that precise moment, his dog, which had been left at Highclere Castle, near Newbury, howled inconsolably and died. The Old Zoologist doesn't know what to make of a story like that and I don't think I do either, but I am prepared to believe that the bond between a dog and a man can be so strong that anything could happen – especially if the dog was a Labrador.

Normally, I do not whine or whimper much because those noises usually express dissatisfaction but I can't help whining if I see a pheasant. This seems to irritate the Chap and his shooting friends, though I cannot understand why. The whole purpose of a shooting expedition is to get the pheasants and I am only letting the shooters know that they are there.

I also occasionally make a little whimper when I see a dog with which I would like to be friendly and the Chap won't let me go.

Finally there is one special sound in Doggish that I make only when I am very pleased indeed, when we are about to go out or when the Boss is scratching my rump. It is a deep throaty sound, 'Wah, wah, wah,' as though I am really trying to say something in English. The Boss says it is sexy and she may be right.

Quite a repertory of sounds, I suggest, and all with meanings which the human members of my pack, as well as other dogs, can comprehend – as the existence of this book bears witness.

There is an African breed of dog called the basenji which is barkless. I feel truly sorry for it, though perhaps it thinks, 'Why keep a man and bark?' On the other hand being quiet may help to protect it from leopards who like it for dinner. My chap had a friend who lived in a bungalow on the outskirts of Nairobi. A leopard crept into the house, killed the Labrador which was asleep on its bed, carried it into the garden and ate it. Not a sound was heard. It was another case of the dog that didn't bark. Sad, but a dog's life is full of surprises!

As in most relationships, the long hours of communion between me and my couple are mainly quiet, at least until I hear something or get bored and feel like making a diversion.

Sometimes I think it is just as well that I cannot speak the human tongue because it would not make for good relations, especially if I was prone to that human imperfection, gossip. I might make comments which I would regret – as so many humans do – for I have noticed that, while we constantly have to put up with criticism for our behaviour, humans find it hard to take. This does not mean that I cannot understand human speech. On the contrary, I know quite a few words, some of which I have listed in a previous chapter. It has been falsely put about by some scientists that we don't really comprehend words spoken to us but are only interpreting the gestures accompanying them. The classic tale, repeated in many books, is that if a dog is told, 'Go to your box!' with the box being pointed at, it will still go if the command is, 'Hole in your socks!' Well that wouldn't work with me. I can definitely understand words even when I cannot see the person saying them. I respond sharply to the word 'Dog' or anything with dog in it, like 'Dogger Bank' when spoken on the radio. When I am on the river in summer, trout fishing with my Chap, I thrust my body through the thick border of great hairy willowherb, hemp agrimony, comfrey and purple loosestrife to see what is happening to his fly as it floats on the water. I cannot see the Chap at all but he only has to say, 'Come out,' and out I come. I also respond smartly to 'Grub up!' even if I am in another room. It is the same with 'All gone' when I have had the last bit of toast or the last dog-choc. Immediately, I know that there is no more and act accordingly. As for 'Pussy!' the Boss has only to say it to send me racing into the garden, hackles up and ready for action. Indeed there are some words, like 'bone', 'lead' and 'out', which I understand so well, however they are spoken, that the couple have to spell them if they do not want me to become prematurely excited.

The calls which shepherds make to their dogs are fully understood, as anyone can see who watches them at work, either in the open or on television, while the communication between dog and dog, when two are working together, is obvious.

There is further evidence that we can understand English. When a dog is exported to a country with a foreign language it is confused for quite a while, though it is usually smart enough to learn the new words quite quickly.

Admittedly, the intonation – the way words are spoken – has a lot to do with my response but isn't it one-up to our intelligence that we can interpret it? The way the Chap or the Boss says 'Dido!', or the other names they sometimes call me, speaks volumes. We can even learn to respond to different tones of whistle.

A lot of what my Chap and the Boss say to me is gobbledegook in canine terms but I can understand most that matters to me. And, of course, their gestures do help to some degree, as they do with each other. In fact, the longer I spend in their company, the more I am astonished by the extent to which they communicate by nods, shakes, arm waves, grunts and other exclamations in spite of the pride humans take in their unique power of speech. Among their gestures which are most meaningful to me are the movements which mean that I am going to be fed – the reach for my stainless-steel bowl and the steps towards the electric tin-opener. The whole process of feeding is such an important aspect of communication to dogs – as it is to you – that it merits a chapter of its own.

11 Food, Glorious Food!

The way to a dog's heart is through its stomach

A balanced diet is as essential to our life and well-being as it is to yours. And, as with you, the act of feeding is a daily delight to be anticipated and enjoyed, along with the unique satisfaction of a full stomach. In addition, feeding is an important form of communication, as it is in your world, though you may never have looked at it consciously in that way. In the wild, when we lived from paw to mouth, the pursuit of food and its enjoyment was a prime function of the pack, and the joint action, the communal chase and the communal feast, in which everyone got a share, was the highlight of the day and cemented the bond between dog and dog. Today, when we are no longer allowed to hunt for ourselves, the provision of food does the same for the bond between dog and man while communal eating is a means of keeping human families and friends in close contact. Not many people enjoy eating on their own, at least not regularly.

I have heard my Chap tell an extraordinary story about an elderly White Russian friend who liked to reminisce about his youth in old Muscovy. He said that while any of the women servants were fair game for the young aristocrats, they would never have dreamed of eating with them. And the women would never have expected them to do so. In short, the act of eating together was on a different plane from the other activity, which would seem to be more intimate. On reflection, we dogs took a similar view. A stray one might steal food from another dog but the sharing of a meal was restricted to the pack, whereas a dog might well mate with any stray bitch, whatever her origin. So maybe the Russian paradox harks back to ceremonial behaviour deeply rooted in the human past. The whole human delight in ritual and ceremony is assuredly related to the essential role which they play in the lives of all social creatures.

I love the ritual, brief as it is, in the preparation of my daily meal, as the Boss, who is my dog-servant, goes through her familiar motions. No sound is sweeter than the burr of the electric tin-opener round about four in the afternoon and it gets the digestive juices flowing. Like all my kind, I salivate copiously to help the food, especially dry biscuit, to slide down into the stomach. Sometimes we dogs get bawled out for 'slobbering' but it really is essential and it is no worse than your horrible habit of blowing your nose into a handkerchief which some people do so frequently, making a dreadful noise in the process.

The feeding ritual helps in establishing and sustaining the bond between the Boss and me, though praise and appreciation are just as important and I also get that from the Chap, who feeds me when the Boss is out.

Though I am usually in the kitchen when the couple eat there, I am never allowed in the dining room. Some dogs are and are so well behaved that they sit in one corner throughout the meal. Regarding one story which I have heard the Chap tell, he might be leg-pulling, though he insists he is not. There was a country house which accommodated a large family and many dogs, some gun dogs, others simply pets, all of which were allowed in the dining room. After dinner, when the ladies quit the dining room to leave the men with their port and stories, all the bitches went with them and the dogs stayed behind.

As the Queen considers tinned pet foods to be good enough for her dogs, both the corgis and Labradors, they are good enough for me, especially as the Boss rings the changes with different flavours like turkey and liver as well as beef. I am also very partial to fish which is supposed to be rich in the special ingredients which build up the brain and there is some theory that the human species owes its big brain to having been mainly a fish-eater in the early days of its evolution. No doubt my ancestors were fed a lot of it by the fishermen in Newfoundland, which might explain why we Labradors are so intelligent. We catch so many trout that I get plenty mixed in with my food, fresh in the summer, and from the deep freeze in winter.

I am also very partial to tripe and that may hark back to our hunting days when internal organs were a delicacy.

As the couple eat out quite a lot and never have me far from their minds, I sometimes experience exotic foods brought home in plastic 'doggy bags'. By and large, I like Chinese and Italian food but not Indian, which tends to be too 'hot' for my tongue, while Mexican was an experiment I hope they will never repeat. The Chap calls Mexican food 'Montezuma's Revenge' and I know what he means. It even killed the grass on the lawn!

A 'dog's dinner' means something unpleasant but mine never is. It is served in a clean, shiny bowl and I am never given food labelled as 'Unfit for human consumption', as some are on the assumption that one man's poison is another dog's meat. Why should we be treated as second-class citizens? I even

111

get brewer's yeast tablets and oil to keep my coat glossy.

Hot food is unnatural for a dog, though much of our freshly killed food must have been quite warm. I don't like it straight from the fridge either, though I suppose that in the wild we chewed at frozen carrion when we were driven to it.

My Chap asked a Jewish lady whether dogs in Jewish homes had to be given kosher meat. She said that it was not necessary because dogs weren't circumcised, whatever that may mean. However, it may be that in really orthodox Jewish homes any non-kosher meat would not be allowed to enter the establishment, not even in tins.

The Boss is right to give me just one big meal a day, rather than two small ones. My stomach is designed to take in the day's food at one go. She ensures that I do not get more than I should, which would make me fat and lazy. A dog that is too fat not only seems to have a head too small for its body but can't run or is not inclined to. Some dogs get so fat that the vet has to prescribe low-calorie diets for them and 'slim-line' dog foods have now appeared on the market. As with humans, carrying too much weight can cause heart problems, arthritis, liver disease and other dangerous conditions. I hear that there are even 'Fido fat-farms', where overweight dogs can be sent to be slimmed down through diet and exercise. No doubt this is costly for the owners but they have themselves to blame for their own lack of willpower in being too indulgent. It is no coincidence that fat people tend to have fat dogs. Part of the problem is that they use their dogs as dustbins to dispose of any scraps as they arise and, undignified though it may sound, most dogs do not mind it at all.

Our trouble is that where food is concerned our old instinct overrules good sense and always will. In the wild our ancestors had to grab what they could and swallow it quickly. They never knew when the next meal might or might not come. We still do the same and rarely refuse a titbit. We are always hungry or appear to be and if, by accident, you feed us twice we will always eat it. The simple truth is that most of us eat until the stomach is fully expanded, and it can expand a great deal. Only then do the hunger pangs really subside. This has been demonstrated in experiments on canine digestion, no doubt carried out with the best of human intentions but also to satisfy human curiosity. Scientists inserted a balloon into a dog's stomach and as soon as they inflated it the dog ceased to feel hungry. When they let it down the dog was prepared to eat.

So what you call greed for food we would call prudence. While a big wolf can eat a stone of meat at a sitting I get only one pound. So when I have emptied my bowl I usually push it around on the patio making a noise to indicate that I would like some more. I never get it but a dog has to live in hopes. (My bowl is always picked up and washed as soon as I have finished because so many home accidents are caused by feeding and water bowls being left where people can trip over them.)

Because of the former danger that our food might be seized and gobbled up by others in the pack we are constructed by physiology and habit not only to eat a lot but to bolt it. It is no coincidence that you say that we 'wolf' our food. It is, in fact, a sign of a healthy dog. We are gluttons, which just means voracious eaters, rather than greedy, which is more of a human attribute. You have your share of gluttons, too, and, though the Chap is reasonably slim, the Boss is always going on at him for eating too quickly. I think her real objection is that the meal, which has taken so long to prepare, is over so soon.

113

We are in no danger of suffering from indigestion even though we bolt our food in such a hurry. One of the reasons that you do is because your digestive organs all hang the wrong way as a consequence of your upright stance. Though we eat the same kinds of food you could never eat yours out of a bowl on the ground as we do because your jaws are the wrong shape and your tongue is too short. Sparing no effort to savour what a dog's life is really like the Chap tried – with stew not dog food – and ended up a fearful mess.

It is because primitive man had hands and the wit to make a skin bag that he developed the habit of having several meals each day. He could take food back to his encampment and did not have to stuff himself on the site of a kill, as we did. We could swallow a little more food than we needed and then regurgitate it for the nursing females and cubs back in the dens but that was all.

While there are so many fat dogs that low-calorie pet food is now on the market, obesity due to over-eating is far more prevalent in the human species and gluttony can be every bit as compulsive as it is with us. The Chap knows one man who over-eats to such an extent that when he reached 30 stones in weight his doctor sewed his mouth up as a last resort and fed him little else but water through a tube. How obscene! It shouldn't happen to a man. Anyway, it did not do much good because, after a few days, the man cut the stitches and gorged himself.

Even if you regard some of us as both gluttonous and greedy we would never breed beyond the available food supply and bring malnutrition and famine on ourselves, a criminal error being committed by your species on a massive scale. If it continues there will be no room for dogs or for yourselves. Even in Britain and similar 'developed' countries, there are so many humans that the food supply can be sustained

114

only by highly artificial methods of farming which are poisoning your lakes and rivers.

Because we bolt our food, the sense of taste does not play such a part as it does with you chewers and suckers. Provided it passes muster by the nose we swallow it. If it smells good it is good. Even with you, taste is considerably mixed up with smell because odour particles reach the inner nose from inside the mouth. But our tongues, which are much longer than they look, can taste salt, sweet, sour and bitter and we soon spit something out we don't like. I did not really taste salt until I was taken to the seaside and tried to bite the waves. Ugh! And I did not really taste bitter until I found a quince in the garden and used it as a ball, though not for long. Ugh! again.

The way I can hide a tablet in my mouth so that it is invisible always baffles the Chap. If he has given me a pill which I am determined not to take he holds my jaws to make me swallow and then opens my mouth to make sure it has gone. Then, after a few moments, I eject it. The least he should do is to wrap it up in something worth swallowing. Even then I sometimes defeat him, though he usually wins in the end.

I know one or two dogs which have been forced to be vegetarians by being put on dog-meal free from meat. They seem to be quite well on it but such a diet cannot be natural with teeth like I've got. The big ones are not called 'carnassial' – flesh-tearers – for nothing. My whole anatomy is typical of a carnivore. The hydrochloric acid in my stomach is strong enough to dissolve bones quickly and my short intestine is not really fitted for much vegetable matter. This is proved by what happens to the peanuts which I cannot resist when they fall out of the dispensers hanging from the bird table. Unless I chew them, which I rarely do, nothing happens and the birds get them in the end, if you see what I mean.

Some people who have been overly motivated by the horror of cruelty to animals urge everybody to become vegetarians, but if people are to be condemned for eating flesh, then so am I and every other naturally carnivorous creature. If the 'Animal Rights' radicals ever succeed with men and women they will then have to go to work on the lion and the wolf!

Being naturally carnivorous is something else which dogs and humans share, and another common feature probably stems from it – our mutual tendency to be aggressive. The Chap expresses it by saying that there will be wars as long as there are dog fights.

For an occasional change, I get a few big soya-bean pellets added to my meat. They are pleasantly crunchy but I would not like to subsist on them. Poor vegetarian dogs which do! They never even get a bone, one of the joys of canine existence and really necessary, I think, when otherwise, with all the soft foods we get, we hardly have any need to use our teeth at all. Small wonder that some dogs have need of dental hygiene with even liver-flavoured toothpaste being marketed for the purpose!

I am rationed to two or three bones a week – never a poultry bone, which is too sharp – because the Chap says that while chewing on bone helps to keep my teeth free of what dentists call plaque, too many would wear them down prematurely. I wouldn't like that but what is better than attending to a juicy bone on a lawn in the sunshine – especially a smelly marrow bone into which I can insert my tongue from both ends? Perhaps, the Chap is more worried about the plants I might dig up while burying a lot of bones!

I suppose wolves buried bones and any other left-overs against the day when food might be scarce. Anyway, it's fun doing it. Sometimes I forget where a bone is buried, like squirrels forget where they have hidden nuts. What a pity that bones can't grow like forgotten nuts do. Usually I get a bone when I am going to be left alone for a while. They give it to me on the lawn and then creep out of the front door. As though I didn't know!

I also like using a small bone as a gobstopper – something to roll round and rattle in the mouth rather than provide any sustenance, perhaps like some people chew gum. Quite often I offer it to my Chap but he never seems to want it, though he does appreciate the gesture.

I also get a few other extras. The first is my morning taste of milk in the Chap's bowl when he has finished his cereals. We usually breakfast together after he has taken the Boss's equally meagre breakfast to her in bed. With her safely upstairs – she disapproves of titbits – I get the cereal dregs with some extra milk. She allows him two eggs a week, rationed in the interest of his arteries – and then we share a couple of rounds of toast, which, fortunately, tend to be 'doorsteps' when he has cut them. The signal I wait for is the crunch when he starts cutting the toast into 'soldiers'. I like it when he throws a bit of toast or bread and I can catch it in flight. It is quite a remarkable piece of co-ordination of mouth and eye – you try it! I always know when I have had my lot at breakfast because he announces, 'All gone!', another English phrase I understand, as I demonstrate by my immediate departure from the table.

Most days I get a little bonus when the birds knock bits of bread off the bird table. The Boss bawls me out for nicking the food left to attract the thrushes, robins and blackbirds but, surely, the dogs can eat of the crumbs which fall from the master's bird table!

In the autumn I can indulge my sweet tooth privately by having a go at the blackberries growing round the back of the garage. I can sense the ripe ones with my nose and they pull off very easily so there are very few left at my height when the Boss goes to pick them. I

am, of course, doing the bush a good turn; the seeds
end up deposited, often far away, and neatly packaged
in their own manure. Isn't Nature wonderful? I don't
know if wolves eat blackberries but I believe that foxes
do, as they eat grapes in vineyards. I see a lot of wild
blackberries on our walks in the late summer but I
don't bother with them. They are not nearly as juicy
as the Boss's in the garden. Another fruit I love is ripe
plums and I have to jump high for them. I spit the
stones out, like humans do, and some of them may
eventually germinate. I wonder if that was what clever
Nature intended, though perhaps the stone of a wild
plum is small enough to pass through the body.

I get a few cooked vegetables – leftovers – mixed in
with my food, but the green stuff I take in with fair
regularity is grass which I can't digest as such but
seems to assist my digestion. I choose the blades I
want with great deliberation and bite them off with
care because their edges can be very sharp, being
fortified with silica – the stuff that makes glass. A cut
tongue would not be pleasant at all. Sometimes I eat
it when my stomach tells me there is something amiss
inside, such as a dangerously sharp piece of bone.
The grass quickly makes me sick and the danger is
resolved. I was involved in a potentially much more
dangerous incident with grass which so impressed the
Chap that he loves telling the story. But I will reserve
that possibly unique experience for a little chapter on
its own.

Round about 9.00 p.m., though sometimes later if
there are guests, I get my ration of dog-chocs and can
indulge my sweet tooth again. The Chap is forever
wondering why dogs love chocolate, as it is hardly
a natural food for them when few, if any, of our
ancestors had access to the cocoa bean. The sweetness
is the likeliest answer because we probably ate sweet
berries when these were available. Tame foxes also

like dog-chocs and tame wolves might do, too, if offered them. Anyway, I think it makes sense for a chocolate dog to like them and, come to that, why do humans like chocolate when it is not natural for them either? My Chap is a chocoholic with a cupboard full of bars, Walnut Whips and Turkish Delights. In my opinion there is a lot of nonsense talked about 'natural' food. Take milk, for example. Most people think of it as intensely 'natural', coming, as it does, straight from a farm. It is natural for little calves all right and maybe for puppies, but for adult humans or grown-up creatures of any kind it could hardly be more unnatural. People and, through their habit, dogs and cats, are the only adult creatures which drink milk. A bowl of milk is not to be barked at but it simply is not 'natural'.

The only natural drink for us is water and we need a plentiful supply of it. You humans, who are used to drinking liquids out of a receptacle and having the help of gravity in swallowing them, don't appreciate what a feat it is for us to lap up water from ground level at the rate we can, just with our tongues. After observing me closely to see how my tongue moved, the Chap tried it as one of his down-to-dog experiences but with little success. Then you can't teach an old man new tricks, can you?

Though we don't enjoy doing it we can go for several days without water or food without suffering serious harm. This is a hangover from our wolf days and explains those stories about dogs being lost down caverns and pipes for days and emerging unscathed. Recently the Boss read out a newspaper story about a little Jack Russell, called Judy, which survived after being trapped underground for five weeks. She lost so much weight that she became thin enough to get near the mouth of a rabbit hole and bark until people came and dug her out.

It is a useful capability but it does not work in very hot conditions when we can dehydrate very quickly. If we go on panting to lose heat from our lungs and mouths we also lose water. So we can soon be in grave trouble if we are left for long in a car on a hot day, even with windows open. You wouldn't leave a dog in a tropical hothouse and that is what a car quickly becomes. If we have to be left for a short time we should have easy access to a bowl of water and we need an occasional sip on all long car journeys. It is common to see people pull up at a pub to slake their thirst without thought for the poor dog.

People are often baffled when we prefer puddle water to the nice clean tap water you provide. The answer, as a rule, is that there is no chlorine in it. If you can smell chlorine in your tap water think what it is like to us – like a gas attack! Actually pure water is not so attractive either. It has no taste and, because of the way we have to lap, our drink is one of the few things we have time to taste.

I suppose that in winter my wolf ancestors had to eat snow – which may explain why instinctively I sometimes bite at it, though I don't swallow it.

The Chap has tried me out with all sorts of other drinks that go down human gullets. I don't like that fizzy bottled water which tickles my nose. I do not like champagne for the same reason. I don't like wine, beer or spirits. And I don't fancy a 'dog's nose', which, I understand, is a mixture of beer and gin. Alcohol might make me tipsy and in a man's world a dog needs her wits about her.

It is an extraordinary comment on human society that most of you find yourselves incapable of coping with life without daily recourse to alcohol. This has been true of all your civilizations in all parts of the world down the ages. The main individual goal of a dog, or any other sensible creature, is to remain in good health and keep on living, yet, in addition to polluting your bloodstream and brain with alcohol, millions of you pollute your lungs with smoke, reducing your well-being and life span in the process. You can be in no doubt what it all does to you but you go on doing it. We have never needed such crutches to cope with life and to be happy. The only crutch we need is you.

If only humans could really appreciate how they look and sound to a stone-cold sober dog when they have had a few drinks! When they are hungover they even try to bring us into it, jokingly, by saying that the best cure is another drink and calling it 'a hair of the dog that bit me'. Of course, as usual, it is humans who bite themselves. Only they would be foolish enough to go on pickling their own livers.

12 To Sleep, Perchance to Dream

Sweet are the slumbers of the virtuous dog

One of the joys of living is to sleep after a good meal. It makes good physiological sense because it means that blood which would otherwise be used by the muscles can be devoted to digestion. Perhaps sleep is particularly necessary for animals with a very full stomach, though I am prepared to forego it for a walk or any other action. I am sure that sleep after big meals is sensible practice for humans, too, and both the Chap and the Boss believe in a half-hour siesta after lunch, with the telephones off the hook. I have not been fed then but I have got into the habit of going to my seat in the conservatory or in the car and lying doggo while they lie manno.

A nap at any time poses no difficulty for me, especially after a hard morning with a bone. We are not diurnal creatures like humans, needing one long sleep at night and staying awake all day. We are twenty-four-hour creatures conditioned to be active by day or night, being so less dependent on our eyes than you are. So, like a good soldier, a dog naps when it can. We do our best to conform to your way of life but please understand if we are sometimes a bit more active during the night than you would prefer.

Some animals like antelopes are so permanently afraid of being attacked that they dare not do anything else but doze and you can never creep up on them. Wolves and wild dogs probably need to sleep 'with one eye open'. So the fact that we can just curl up and sleep soundly in your presence without fear is, perhaps, the frankest expression of our trust in you. We are even prepared to sleep stretched out or in the even more vulnerable position of being on our backs with our legs in the air. My Chap can often creep up on me if I am asleep but not if I am just dozing, as I often am when I am bored.

Fortunately, we do not have to put up with being bored like you do. I know that when the Chap is at some dinner or function he frequently says to himself 'What the hell am I doing here?' But he just has to bear with it because of the pretence demanded by your code of manners when he would much rather get up and leave. We never put up with being bored for long. We either disappear or go to sleep. As I am often bored this means that I am lumbered with more slumber than I really need. However, like you, I rather enjoy it, so long as I am not missing any action. I am happy to be awakened any time for action but dislike being roused for no good reason and quickly go to sleep again. I never suffer from insomnia, though thunder can give me a disturbed night.

By nature we like to curl up into a ball, hiding our most vulnerable part – our soft underbelly. I may look silly when I go round and round before I settle, as though making an imaginary nest, and some wiseacres think I am knocking imaginary grass down, as I would in the wild, but I have a different theory. I think I am going through the instinctive motions of trying to sense the direction of the wind to make sure that my emergency alarm system – my nose – would be facing it while I slumbered. My business end – my jaws – would also present itself to an aggressor. I don't do it when I sit down outside but I always know which way the wind is blowing there. When I am inside I don't. Whatever the reason, it is one of several inherited habits with which we have to comply before life is comfortable for us. If you think about it, you go through quite a ritual before you can settle down in bed, with all that undressing, washing, combing, toothbrushing and, in the case of females, the cosmetic routine.

For proper sleep I like an allotted place, like you do, and in fact I have two – an armchair in the conservatory, the best location for guarding the house, and a giant beanbag in another room. I don't like those plastic containers with sides and have firmly declined one belonging to a previous resident. Maybe I suffer from claustrophobia, as I know that some dogs do, or maybe it's just that I can't stretch out properly. The conservatory chair was supposed to be my day bed but when I realized that the heat was on there all night, for the canary as well as the plants, I switched and use the beanbag for my daytime rest.

Normally I am not permitted to sleep in the bedrooms, though many dogs are, but when the Boss was away for a week the Chap allowed me on the bed to observe my movements while I was asleep. Humans move a lot in their sleep and he wanted to see if dogs do. He had no difficulty in staying awake because of my weight on the bed and so many little touches of Dido in the night. It seemed that I moved too much for him to want to repeat the experiment, which increased his wonder why so many dogs are allowed to sleep on the bed. The Chap knew one old couple who always slept together with two Labradors on the bed and he had often wondered how they had managed to get any sleep. After his experiment that mystery deepened.

According to the Queen Mother's corgi, Ranger, who recently described a day in his life in a magazine, he always sleeps on the Royal bed. The Queen's dogs have never given tongue in print but my Chap spent a few shooting weekends with the Prince of Wales when he was younger. Prince Charles, as he was then, had a black Labrador which always slept in his bedroom, perhaps as part of the security arrangements. He probably was not allowed on the bed but loud cries of 'You!' indicated that he sometimes disobeyed the Royal command.

Ranger confessed that while staying at the Castle of Mey, the Queen Mum's Highland hide-away, he was temporarily banned from the bedroom because of a bout of snoring. This is an unfortunate habit we also share with you. It is caused by the vibration of soft tissues at the back of the mouth cavity and we both have them. If the back of the soft palate comes too close to the throat lining, as it can in certain sleeping positions, it forms a narrow tube and when air is forced through it during breathing the soft tissues flap and flutter like a reed in a wind instrument. My Chap is fairly good at it and often wakes with a snort when he is having his siesta and lying on his back on the sofa. I am told that I snore occasionally but am not too bad, though of course, like humans, dogs tend to snore more when they get older, so my time may come. The Chap once wrote a newspaper article quoting a famous ear, throat and nose surgeon who alleged that the dog is the only domestic animal which snores. It brought 96 letters from incensed owners of snoring cats!

Another habit we share, along with many other creatures, is yawning, which is said to be an automatic effort to offset tiredness by increasing the amount of oxygen in the lungs. When my Chap starts yawning so do I and vice versa, though nobody knows why. He once read that some people are so susceptible to a suggestion of a yawn that you can make them yawn by opening and shutting your hands in front of them. He has tried this on me several times but it never works.

There seems to be no doubt among scientists that dogs share your habit of dreaming and do so regularly. Nobody doubts that a baby can dream – just watch its expressions while it sleeps – so why should anyone doubt that we dream, just because we can't tell anybody about it?

In one experiment scientists put a piece of sausage in front of a sleeping dog's nose and watched it go through the motions of chewing in its sleep. The Chap tried it with me but I wasn't properly asleep and I just opened my eyes and ate it.

In another test scientists put pine needles in front of a sleeping hound which had been hunting in an Austrian forest and then watched him go through the motions of excitement. We don't go into pine woods very often and leaves and twigs taken from our walks didn't work with me and were not popular with the Boss because they made a mess on the carpet. Still the Chap is quite certain that I do dream regularly.

When humans dream, and only then, their eyeballs jerk rapidly under the closed lids so that scientists can tell for certain when dreaming is taking place. By watching my eyelids when I am asleep – I sometimes catch him doing it – the Chap has convinced himself that my eyeballs also undergo this rapid oscillation, so I must be dreaming. Well, of course I am but I don't dream in pictures like you do. I dream mainly in smells which is why my nostrils twitch so much during sleep. My Chap says that I also smile and wag my tail when I am asleep, indicating a happy dream. Further, I sometimes awake with a start as humans do when they have been dreaming vividly.

The scientists claim to recognize four type of dog dreams: running, which is also common in humans, feeding, snarling and barking. (We don't have sex dreams but then we are not ridden by it like you are, though I can't speak for male dogs. Nor are our dreams due to the repressed desires of puppyhood.) I don't do much snarling in my sleep but I bark occasionally and then my voice is different because it comes out through almost closed jaws.

With running-and-chasing dreams my paws move and my muscles are so tense that they sometimes jerk and wake me up. The Chap, who is loaded with useless information, calls them myoclonic jerks and gets them himself.

Why do we need to dream? Dreaming seems to be a necessary part of sleep for both our species though nobody seems to know why. It may be the cerebral computer riffling through a lot of the useless material stored in its memory and getting rid of some of it. But there must be more to it than that.

Unfortunately, like a lot of humans, I can't remember my dreams but the Chap assumes that, like him, I get occasional nightmares. I certainly have daydreams when I am half-dozing in the car, or at least I've heard the Chap say I do. He also says that I probably experience hallucinations like healthy humans do on occasion. I would not know if I did because an hallucination looks as real as reality itself and I could not tell the difference. If I do sometimes hallucinate I wonder if I do it mainly in smells. It might account for those rare occasions when I think something is there and then find nothing. The Chap says it could also explain stories about dogs seeing or hearing ghosts, or perhaps smelling them, because if they can be seen and heard they should smell as well. In fact those which are supposed to come out of graves and tombs should smell rather a lot.

Dreams or no dreams, like the few humans I have known intimately, I do not bound out of bed immediately I awaken. In fact I feel bog-eyed for a while and spend quite a while coming to terms with reality. On some days when the bed 'pulls' I just don't feel like getting up which, no doubt, is the result of watching human habits, but when the Chap comes down to pull the papers out of the letter-box I hear the click and wander out to greet him and follow him upstairs. I am usually allowed on the connubial bed in the morning after the tea has been drunk and while the newspapers are being perused. Then I am the dog in the middle, a position I like for a short while until I decide to make it clear that it is time the Chap moved himself.

I do take umbrage on the occasions when I am forbidden to get on the bed, being sent instead to my bedroom chair and later called to the bed when it suits them. I usually go but sometimes I let them know I am not best pleased at this display of species discrimination by staying curled up on my chair, which happens to be very comfortable. They retaliate by calling me 'Lady Dido', 'Lady Di', 'Queen Dido' and 'Her Majesty' but I don't mind that at all. (What I don't like is being called 'dog' – 'Watch out, dog!' and so on. It's like a gentleman being called 'Fellow!' The Chap often calls me Sheika, accidentally after his late ridgeback, but I quite like that, knowing how much he loved her. A woman wouldn't, though, would she?)

One of the nicest of our rituals occurs at the other end of the day – the tuck-up, when the Chap ensures that we are all safely locked in, the security system is working, the dog-doors are unlocked, that I have water and, after being out in the garden, am comfortably on my chair or on my beanbag. It is then that any memory of the day's minor fall-outs is washed away – his irritation never lasts long – and we have always made it up before we part for the night.

Sometimes, though not too often, when I can't sleep and am bored in the night, I run out into the garden and the anti-burglar lights and the howler all go on, for I know just where to position myself to do this. Then I bark and down comes my Chap in his pyjamas brandishing a great antique policeman's truncheon and we go round the house together. That's always good for a canine laugh, which I can do silently with my tail. Of course he can't be sure that there wasn't some intruder trying the padlocked gate so I always get away with it, and upstairs he goes, chuntering, 'The devil's got into that dog recently.' Anyway, he should put up with my occasional jokes because I have to put up with his idea of humour, such as his awful joke that the best dog of all is the hot dog because it feeds the hand that bites it!

If I feel lonely in the night I search for a shoe, a towel or anything else I can find belonging to the other pack members and have it close by me on my bed. It has to be in contact with me to serve as a comforter, like a child needs to be in touch with its teddy bear or favourite blanket. On occasion when, perhaps, I feel particularly isolated, I may collect as many as four or five shoes if they are handy, and the Chap thinks this is a bit kinky. But this deep-seated need is not as infantile as it seems. When the Chap and the Boss go away they always take some small pillows with them. They like the extra comfort but psychologists suspect that the link with home helps them to sleep better in a strange bed. Maybe, as a symbolic link with the missing pack, a shoe or a towel does the same for me.

Experiments on humans and many animals have proved the obvious – as scientists spend so much time doing – that regular sleep recharges the canine computer in our heads and is essential for good health, a subject I will deal with next.

13 Fitness, not Fatness

Health is the first good lent to dog

According to the Chap, who was once the medical correspondent of a newspaper, only four fads for improving health and life span have stood the test of time – avoiding excess weight, taking regular exercise, giving up smoking and restricting the intake of alcohol. The last two are of no interest to me but the first two undoubtedly apply to dogs. The sheer effort of carrying around excess fat, day after day, reduces life span and all we medium-sized and small dogs should heed the fact that large breeds tend to age quickly and die rather young. Being semi-humanized, the average life span of dogs in general has increased over the last few decades, like man's has but, as with most things, there are penalties, such as heart problems.

Fortunately, the Boss is weight-conscious herself and as soon as my figure begins to look flabby I am put on short commons. I don't like it at the time but she has my interests at heart. 'Don't let the body go' is good advice for dogs as well as humans. Otherwise old age creeps up before its time.

Next to avoiding obesity the best antidote to heart trouble is exercise and most of us get far too little for our good. I really need to walk about four miles a day to stay healthy and keep my muscles and posture in tone. Except on days when we are fishing or out on a shoot, I don't get that much. We have to conform to your habits and timetable and you now spend so little energy controlling your environment – even your car windows are electric – that you are progressively disinclined to move. As a result you all suffer from more degenerative diseases because there is nothing like disuse for weakening any system and we are in danger of doing the same.

For me, a 'walk' is always better off a lead, if that is safe, because then I can trot, which is my natural pace – a dog-trot – and run back and forth which increases my mileage. As I will describe later, I am fortunate in getting a fair amount of this free movement. I reckon that I also need the exercise to keep my Chap healthy. It is as important to his heart as it is to mine to make him walk when he'd rather not and I regard that as one of the benefits we dogs bestow on the human race. If I did not badger him until he gets my lead we could both vegetate into becoming fireside creatures, and by nature I am an action animal, as he still is at heart.

I prefer running on grass or in woods but there is also the quite important need for some road work to keep my claws short.

After a good bout of exercise, which is such fun in itself, comes the special pleasure of relaxation and sleep when one is physically tired, a joy we both experience.

While I reckon that we are a pretty tough species, we are susceptible to draughts and should not be made to sleep in them, especially when we are wet. This may be because our body temperature – about 101°F – is higher than yours. Just a few degrees can make a big difference to the body's metabolic rate.

Fortunately, we are immune to colds, which the Chap spends so much time trying to dodge but eventually fails. The way the human nose is bunged up by a cold would be tantamount to being temporarily blind for me. When I sneeze I am simply clearing my nose from some natural obstruction, which is always necessary when smell is so vital to us. If you watch a dog carefully you will see that it sneezes with its mouth shut while a human has to open the mouth, emitting a cloud of germ-laden vapour. Because of the human body's erect posture, the air breathed out has to go all the way from the lungs up the nose and then down it to get out. So when the air is under high pressure in a sneeze it takes the easier way out – through the mouth. We always have a straight run, breathing or sneezing. Another one-up to dogdom!

Damp conditions are supposed to cause rheumatism and it is common for dogs to suffer from it. I have seen some which wear copper collars to ward off rheumatism but the Chap says that they make no sense and if I had a copper collar, as well as my tick collar and ordinary collar, I would begin to look like one of those giraffe-necked women. He is also opposed to having me dressed up like a dog's breakfast in the gaudy coats which have become a fashion craze, being designed more to match their mistresses' autumn and winter outfits than to keep their wearers warm.

We are susceptible to diseases to which you are immune, like distemper and hard pad, but most of these can be prevented by injections which we should have regularly and should never be postponed if you really value us.

Cleanliness is an innate part of dogliness and, provided we are kept in clean surroundings, there is probably no cleaner creature on earth, a dirty dog being rare. There is nothing we can do about dog fleas, but with sprays and powders you can see to it that we never have them for long, so long as you also remember to spray our bedding. We can't do much about ticks either without your help. They are horrid bloodsuckers which we pick up on our walks, especially from any place where sheep have been. Their heads need to be touched with a drop of petrol on a fine brush and then they can be lifted out and destroyed. If you try to twist them out the jaws will remain in the skin and produce a nasty sore.

When we shuffle our backsides along the ground it is not a sign that we have worms, as commonly believed. Our anal glands, which are part of our scent apparatus, are giving us trouble and we need hard food like bones to give them some natural massage. No dog should have worms these days when there are simple medicines to keep them free from them.

While we may be more susceptible than you to cuts from horrible man-made hazards like barbed wire and food cans the healing power of our flesh is much better.

Like you, I have off days when I don't feel as active as usual and some when I feel as sick as a man. Maybe the weather has something to do with it but, whatever it is, a few blades of the right grass usually puts it right. When I am off colour I like to be on my own because I feel uneasy if I am not. I suppose that I remain instinctively aware of the old pack law that the infirm have to be sacrificed in the general interest. So I need to hide myself and the fact that I do so is a sign that I am not well. Drinking excessive amounts of water and, of course, being off my food are other signs. As I have pointed out, we do not feel pain as intensely as you do so we do not do much groaning or whining when we are ill.

There is no truth in the idea that a wet nose spells good health in a dog while a warm dry nose is not so good. A lot depends on the air temperature. The same applies to warm ears, which some owners regard as a bad sign. We get rid of excess body heat through our ears and they are bound to feel warm then.

I literally go 'off colour' when I moult because the dead hair looks lighter and loses its natural gloss. Like your skin, mine is a good indicator of my general health. Regular brushing, which I quite enjoy, is the best skin tonic.

My advice to humans in general is to keep an eye on us but not to get too worried about the odd symptoms. Common symptoms have common causes yet my couple are inclined to rush me to the vet at the slightest sign of medical trouble while they put off going to the doctor when their own symptoms are far worse. I know the vet means well but I hate going to a surgery. That smell!

One of the greatest dangers we quite heavy dogs face is twisting of the stomach, which killed the Chap's last ridgeback. Not only does it constrict the food canal but puts pressure on the heart and lungs which can be fatal in a couple of hours. I like to jump up, especially to show my excitement when the food is arriving, but the Chap does his best to stop me because of that danger. Twisted gut is a fairly common cause of death in horses and the vet says that it occurs more often than most people know among large dogs.

I am fortunate to be female because, as with humans, we females are more durable than the males and live substantially longer on average. Infant mortality is greater among male puppies and the female pup has a longer expectation of life. A Labrador in Britain once lived to be just short of its twenty-seventh birthday, though I suppose some of the small breeds have lived even longer. Much depends on one's parents. If they are long lived, their offspring can expect the same good fortune, barring accidents, of course. Sadly, some parents can pass on disabilities which can lead to a dog's premature end. One of them, hip displacement, is common in some strains of Labrador but fortunately not in mine.

As with humans, our general life expectancy seems to be growing and dogs which would have died or been put down are now surviving with heart pacemakers, heart valves and hip replacements. I reckon that this is only fair considering that many of these life-saving operations devised for humans were first performed on dogs.

Apart from having the right parents, which has much to do with health and longevity, a dog needs luck to remain healthy and all of one piece in this dangerous world. More than 50,000 road accidents are caused by dogs in Britain each year with most of the dogs being killed or maimed. Many are strays which have been turned out or have run away from bad homes and in almost all cases the owners are to blame. Thousands of dogs are put down because they bite humans or livestock – again usually because owners do not keep them under control. So the prime luck is in acquiring a good home with caring and understanding people, and too many dogs are manned by bad luck in that respect. There are unlucky dogs just as there are unlucky people. So far, my luck has held out and I do not intend to push it, though my Chap frequently tells me that I do.

It would seem, however, that excessive attachment to a Chap can, on occasion be fatal to a faithful dog. Unlike so many humans, we are not hypochondriacs but there are many well-attested accounts of dogs quickly pining to death when their masters died or left them. Scientists now believe that they know the cause – the extreme stress can so damage the body's complicated hormone system that it becomes self-destructive and either causes fatal shock or destroys all immunity to infection. It used to be called 'a broken heart'.

More and more humans, especially men, are having regular health checks so that any problems can be detected and treated early. This is part of a general move towards preventive medicine and I see no reason why it should not be applied to dogs. Indeed, I imagine that specially valuable dogs, like racing greyhounds, are already checked regularly by vets. They are certainly insured against accident or illness and many insurance companies offer cover against veterinary costs for any dogs whose owners care to take out policies. Come to think of it, now that I am a published author, with one paw on the ladder of success, shouldn't the Chap insure me against loss of literary earnings?

14 Crime and Punishment

To err is canine, to forgive humane

All pack animals are born amenable to discipline and have to learn it quickly if they are to survive because without it social life is impossible. Like you, we need and prefer a disciplined life, so long as it is not harsh. Nevertheless, a healthy dog with energy to expend is bound to do some things which you might count as delinquent. Sometimes it is difficult for us to conform as you would like but always remember that no other creature makes such a sustained and generally successful effort to do so. Bear that in mind when you are tempted to chastise us, either manually or verbally, when we fall out of line.

Knowing nothing about sin, morality and ethics are meaningless to us. We do, however, know temptation and it is in both our interests for you to do your best to save us from it, especially by not making food too easily accessible.

Fortunately, I am not a thief and have never been 'in the doghouse' yet on that score, but some dogs, like some humans, are real kleptomaniacs and cannot resist any food that is within possible reach. I gather that nothing was safe from some of my ridgeback predecessors but I believe that they are a notoriously greedy breed. Their behaviour was clearly in the mind of the Boss when she read out the caption on a huge poster advertisement for British Telecom while we were held up in traffic recently. The poster showed an empty place on a table with a message written for a hapless husband by a much tried wife – 'Your dinner is in the dog.' I was quite offended.

Next to temptation, boredom is the commonest cause of canine 'crime' and leads to vandalism, as it does in humans. Recently, when my Chap and I were walking through the village churchyard we caught some young boys chipping the names out of the war memorial with a piece of flint. They seemed nice enough lads and were on holiday and bored stiff. Another group pushed one side of a beautiful old brick bridge into the river. Idle hands get up to mischief and so do idle paws and idle teeth. The scientists call it 'displacement behaviour' and it is a reaction to boredom, frustration and, in the case of only dogs, loneliness which looms large when we are left alone or ignored for hours at a time.

One of my predecessors, a black-eyed springer spaniel called Skipper, had a delinquent way of expressing his boredom – he tore up books. He chose with care because the first one he tore up, from the shelf in the Chap's study labelled 'Military', was called *The Atomic Bomb*. Not many dogs have torn up the atomic bomb! Fortunately, it was an old, man-eared book. (I object to 'dog-eared' when it is man who defaces his books by turning down the pages.) Canine psychiatrists would say that Skipper was simply prone to 'separation anxiety' and lost control when he was left on his own. I'm glad that he is not around to tear up this book before I finish it.

I am not a tearer-up of books. When I am bored I skin tennis balls. I find them much more interesting when I am down to the rubber. The Chap doesn't mind because we find replacements which have floated down the river and collected at the grills by the hatches, the local name for little weirs where the water flow can be controlled.

I suppose that the commonest complaint against dogs is excessive barking, especially at night. This is almost always the result of loneliness. Dogs are left alone for too long, become bored and bark to secure attention or simply to air their feelings and have them heard. The worst barkers are usually those poor creatures who are almost permanently chained up outside. The obvious cure rests in the hands of the owners.

There is one crime in these and many other country parts that is regarded as so serious that it frequently carries the death penalty: the habit of some dogs to go off hunting the local pheasants. Gamekeepers do not like it and some of them are trigger happy. Having heard how the Boss began breeding ridgebacks I can understand why. A friend had a ridgeback bitch as a guard dog on his estate and it got into one of his pheasant pens and killed more than a hundred of them. The Boss resolved its problem by giving it a home where it could not get at any pheasants, though it still killed chickens and ducks, if given a chance.

Chasing sheep is an even more dangerous pastime but I am not allowed to do that either. Biting humans, which has been much in the news lately, is even worse but, as I have said, in nearly all cases it is the owners who are to blame for failing to exercise control. Some of us are mistrustful of strangers, as was necessary in the wild, and while biting them is going too far, a dog is only doing his job if he shows his dislike. Humans would be well advised to take care with anyone a dog dislikes on sight.

On the subject of blame and responsibility there is an increasing fashion to attribute human crime to circumstances beyond the control of the criminal, such as being 'socially deprived'. There are even better grounds for such a liberal view of canine crimes like vandalism, hyperactivity and aggression which can all be due to 'behavioural deprivation'. This simply means that you humans keep us under conditions which make it impossible for us to behave as we need to and would like. Loneliness, lack of exercise and being kept indoors far too long are probably the commonest causes. It can also be argued that some inherited defects caused by 'cosmetic' breeding for the 'fancy' induce behaviour which you dislike.

In my experience there are some odd inconsistencies in human attitudes to our 'crimes'. Take the Chap for instance. In his book it would be a crime if I killed a blackbird in the garden but not if I killed a cat. The Chap happens to dislike cats as much as I do because they kill literally millions of songbirds and he strongly approves when I chase them, while others might regard it as a vice. The sparrowhawk also kills songbirds but when it swoops into the garden to get one he is wildly excited because he happens to like and admire birds of prey. I am sure I would be in dire trouble if I killed the sparrowhawk. Odd, isn't it? I came nearest to testing the depth of the Chap's love when George the canary escaped from his cage and, for a few seconds, we were nose to beak on the floor of the conservatory. The Chap was horrified but I was only being friendly. Or was I?

Though I have heard the Chap say that I am totally without guile and I don't commit many crimes I am prepared to confess to a few vices. I am certainly not popular when I dig holes in the garden, especially if they happen to uproot some choice plant. Sometimes I am not entirely sure why I do it except that it is fun to scrabble in soft earth. On other occasions I have a perfectly valid reason which the Chap is usually slow to understand. Take, for instance, the occasion when I dug up a whole patch of young perennial plants which he had put in so carefully. I could smell something quite irresistible round the roots and it took him some time to realize what it was – bone meal. He wasn't very sharp was he? He has stopped using bone meal now. A pity! The smell was delicious.

I suppose that I must know that it is wrong to dig in his precious borders because I choose a place where the Chap is unlikely to spot it for a few days and by then it will be too late to mete out any punishment. Sometimes, however, he is observant enough to spot mud on my nose and paws and then goes in search of the hole made by what he calls 'the dirty digger'.

He also strongly disapproves when I chase any of the garden birds, especially if the greater spotted woodpecker or the nuthatch happens to be feeding on one of the peanut dispensers, though he appreciates that it is in my inherited nature to chase anything that flies.

To keep canine delinquency in perspective it is only fair to draw attention to the appalling extent of human criminality. Few humans have never broken the law and when conscription was in force the Army reckoned that 10 per cent of the recruits called up would be crooks. Some recent figures showed that about a third of all men commit some crime by the time they are thirty-five. So we do not do too badly and, as a race, we make up for any offbeat behaviour by helping to prevent human crime by serving as guard dogs, drug detectors and anti-riot dogs.

In the context of human crime it is intriguing to compare your predicament with ours in these violent times. Straying dogs could once be guaranteed kicks and blows, especially in towns. Now it is people – females as well as males – who are more likely to suffer savage attack and who need to be on guard against sudden assault.

To warrant fair punishment, humans must know that they were doing wrong and I reckon that, in all equity, that principle should apply to dogs. Much chastisement which is inflicted on dogs is undeserved because it results from failing to understand the limitations in our ability to conform with your requirements, however willing we would like to be. It also serves no purpose unless you are prepared to concede that you sometimes use us as 'whipping dogs' for that all too common human weakness of releasing your own feelings of anger and frustration in violence or verbal abuse – common in the shooting field when a man is shooting badly. When that happens I am a dog of sorrows, for while we have a sense of justice, which in the wild is meted out by the pack leader and in civilized life by the Chap, we are equally well aware that we are being treated unfairly when we are blamed for something we did not do. 'A staff is quickly found to beat a dog' and there is little we can do about it, except get out of the way.

Most people would agree that dogs should not be sent to prison but this is what, effectively, happens to many which are put in kennels for weeks at a time. To a dog which is used to sleeping in a warm house with the family for company this can be like being committed to solitary confinement in a cold cell. Happily some kennels are becoming far-sighted enough to provide canine home comforts – warmth, homely surroundings, comfortable dog beds and, above all, human companionship.

Fortunately for our relationship, all dogs are strong on forgiveness, never bear grudges and remain faithful to the pack and to the pack leader, however harsh or unthinking he may be. There have been tragic cases where gun dogs, following hares or rabbits too closely, have been accidentally shot by their masters and have given a final friendly wag, and even a lick, before expiring. Forgiveness is perhaps the most eloquent expression of our devotion but I know how to ration it to my advantage. It is a powerful weapon. I also know how to beg forgiveness when I have done wrong. On both sides we need to remember that those whom we forgive the most are, or should be, those whom we love the most.

There may be times when, if we are caught in a 'delinquent' act, a slap serves the purpose of showing us that you are withdrawing your affection, which is what hurts us most. But it is no good punishing us long after an offence because our memories are not that long enough for us to associate the retribution with what we might have done.

Even when a canine offender is caught in the act punishment may serve no purpose if the reason for the offence happens to be very strong in the dog's mind. The Chap once caught the Boss's favourite ridgeback killing a tame duck which was sitting on eggs. As this was the fourth offence and he had been waiting to catch her red-toothed, he belaboured her with the dead duck so much that the Boss was in tears. But it did not stop the ridgeback from doing it again. Nor were marital relations improved when he asked the Boss if she would like the duck to make duck paté!

Ridgebacks were originally bred for hunting in Africa, either singly or in packs, being so brave that they were even used for hunting lions! So the poor old girl was only doing what her ancestors had been bred to do, though I admit that killing a duck does not require much courage.

Some of our social peccadilloes spring from our sheer devotion to you. Sometimes, for example, my friendliness runs away with me and I can't resist jumping up to show my pleasure – to the ruination of several pairs of tights. The Chap's efforts to extricate us both socially when I jump up at somebody on our walks invoke various excuses. 'Sorry about that but she's only a puppy,' which patently I am no longer. Or, trading on the better nature of my sex, 'It's all right, it's a bitch. She's very friendly.' Or putting the blame on the victim – 'It's that plastic bag you're carrying that interests her. She thinks there is something in it for her.' And so on, through the whole specious repertory in this ritual of human manners. Only very occasionally does he feel that he has to put on an act of disciplining me by giving me the gentlest tap on my rump with his blackthorn thumbstick and making sure that the offended person observes it.

I am also inclined to jump up to express my jealousy, which is, perhaps, another vice. I definitely don't like it when my Chap makes a fuss of another dog in my presence. What female would? We hate losing face, especially in front of other dogs. And I soon come running to find out what is going on if the Boss makes an excessive fuss of the Chap, which she sometimes does just to tease me. I know that I am top dog but I need reassurance.

It is specially difficult for us to understand when you encourage us to do something which amuses you and then chastise us for doing it at a time when it just does not happen to suit you. Begging for food is an example. It is in our nature to beg because young wolves beg food from their parents. So we do not need much encouragement to beg at the table, which can become a nuisance in your eyes, especially if you have guests.

I have to concede, then, that, remarkable as we dogs are, there are a few unfortunate aspects of our nature that may occasionally break through our reserve. When that happens just remember the words of the poet – 'a dog's a dog for a' that', and that a dog has some natural rights, which I will now expound.

15 The Rights of Dog

If dogkind had wished for what is right,
they might have had it long ago

Recent research into the dog-man relationship by the Companion Animal Research Group at Cambridge University has proved what has long been obvious to us – dogs exert a positively beneficial impact on human well-being, both physical and mental. By inducing their owners to take regular exercise they reduce the risk of heart ailments and improve fitness generally. Their companionship lessens the mental impact of depression, loneliness, boredom and other forms of stress, thereby enhancing the quality of life for millions. While, by nature, we prefer a biggish pack of four, five or even more, there must have been many times in the old days when we were reduced to two. How that couple must have clung together, conscious of how near they were to the dangerous, probably fatal, position of being alone in a savage environment! The same must often have applied to the human pack, threatened by enemies and natural forces. That primitive fear still exists in both of us and is expressed in the way the solitary man or woman and their dog cling together for mutual support. It is in such a situation that our inexhaustible capacity for sympathy achieves its most sublime utility.

This canitarian service to human welfare is on top of the utilitarian benefits which dogs have bestowed through hunting, sheep-herding, retrieving, pulling dogcarts, turning spits, running races, guarding property, guiding the blind, fetching and carrying for the disabled, alerting the deaf, finding victims of earthquakes and avalanches, controlling crowds, tracking criminals, detecting hidden mines and drugs and indulging human vanity by competing in trials and shows. By nature we are dogs of peace, at least I am, yet in times past you trained some of us to be dogs of war – shock troops fitted with collars armed with spikes and knives to slash the legs of enemy cavalry.

In addition there is the contribution made by those millions of dogs used for vivisection, which is such an odious aspect of the canine predicament. Though the medical results may be useful to vets as well as to doctors I find it hard to condone, though the Chap does his best to defend it. Nor, in retrospect, could I approve of the launching of a dog into space, as the Russians did, even though it meant that the dog notched up another first over man by beating him into orbit in what the newspapers called 'The Flying Dog Kennel'. A giant step for mankind, maybe, but not for dogkind because it was never intended to bring the poor creature back to earth and it died, as planned, out there in the cold loneliness of space. Human knowledge can be bought at too high a canine price.

I maintain that the mere fact of our existence as highly developed and sensitive creatures entitles us to certain basic rights, and our enduring service and sacrifices over so many centuries require that entitlement to be formally recognized by human society. What are these canine rights?

It is widely believed that all humans have inalienable rights such as the rights to life, liberty and the pursuit of happiness. Many also subscribe to the belief that all humans are created equal and are 'brothers'. To us dogs, watching human behaviour with objective eyes, most of this is arrant humbug. In the first place, most of the famous and infamous names in history spent their time proving that human rights are very alienable indeed, as still happens in the countries ruled by dictators. As for being created equal, this is as false for people as it is for dogs and nobody, human or canine, really believes it. We are each of us individually unique, physically, mentally, medically and in all other respects, including needs and merits. It takes all sorts of dogs, as well as people, to make a world.

Even if we were born equal we would not remain equal for long. Our natural way of life is based on the existence of a hierarchy in the pack, with one leader to whom deference has to be paid by the others less fitted for that task, in the interest of order and peace. In fact individuality and variability are the basic strengths of both your species and ours and have been responsible for our evolutionary success.

Even the belief that there should be equality of opportunity is a mirage, incapable of fulfilment. The best any of us can hope for is a reasonably fair chance, provided our genes and misfortune have not ruled that out. So I shall not be demanding equality or fair shares but will be honest enough to admit that I am more than happy with the unfair share I am lucky enough to enjoy.

While it is true that in a country like Britain most people enjoy a great deal of freedom and liberty they are still constrained by an increasing number of laws and customs, many of which also apply to us. It is not widely known but I am told that until about 300 years ago dogs could be held caninely responsible for their crimes and were sometimes tried by judges and hanged. They could be convicted of witchcraft and burned at the stake. Some were even excommunicated, though I don't suppose that many dogs had been going to Communion. Such is the wisdom of man, and though his brain cannot have evolved much in that time we do seem to live in slightly more enlightened times. It seems unfair, though, that while capital punishment has been abolished for humans in many countries on the grounds that it is barbaric, dogs are still frequently condemned to death by the courts.

Nevertheless, the last thing we dogs want is liberty. We are much better off being legally a human possession, a chattel if you like, subservient to a human pack leader. Liberty for a dog might mean freedom to roam but it would also mean scrounging in dustbins for food, sleeping rough and being at risk on the roads. Dogs have always been at risk of being run over, even by coaches and carts, but the advent of motor traffic in such vast numbers has made the canine environment infinitely more dangerous. All the liberty we need is reasonable freedom to roam in the household coupled with freedom of speech in the form of a legitimate amount of barking. As intelligent creatures we do have the power of choice and sometimes we should be allowed to exercise it, though usually we are resigned to the fact that, on important issues, we will have to do what you want or, at least, appear to do so. No sensible dog living in a human environment should have any illusions or pretensions about being pack leader and I, for one, know on which side my biscuit is buttered.

I agree that every human being has a natural claim to the pursuit of happiness and this is also a reasonable canine demand. But we shall both be chasing a phantom if we think that happiness is an entity which can be captured and held. Happiness is made up of a lot of separate things which need to go on happening and we must work at them by conscious effort to ensure that they do. If you have a happy nature and reasonable luck they probably will but they will not if you are miserable by temperament, as some humans and dogs undoubtedly are. As for luck, which is so often the dominant factor in all our lives, no Bill of Rights can cater for it.

My realistic Bill of Canine Rights is based on the reasonable claim that as members of the human-canine pack, making a substantial contribution to its welfare, we are entitled to its privileges. So I propose:

1 All dogs should be registered by law, with their own number and their owner's name on a computerized National Register. The number should be tattooed, discreetly, on the inside of each dog's ear, or a tiny silicon chip could be implanted by a vet. That way owners of lost dogs could be quickly notified.

2 Registration should cost a reasonable fee to discourage those who buy puppies and dogs on a whim.

3 The law should require that all changes of ownership be notified to the Register. (Pending the necessary legislation, a voluntary scheme is already being implemented as a privately run project called the National Dog Bureau but, to be really effective, registration needs to be compulsory like car registration.)

4 It should be a fineable offence if an owner can be shown to have deliberately abandoned a dog. (In Britain alone about 1,000 unwanted dogs, originally acquired as pets, are being humanely destroyed *every day*.)

5 I was glad to hear that pit bull terriers and some other breeds developed purely for fighting and, therefore, dangerous to both humans and other dogs, are being phased out of Britain and no more may ever be

imported. Initially, after children had been savaged, the Home Secretary panicked and decreed that the 10,000 or so specimens already here should all be destroyed. Under pressure from dog lovers, however, he backed down and ruled that they could be neutered and muzzled if the owners did not want them put down. I suppose it is possible that this was a bit of a trick. Perhaps the Home Secretary made his first shock announcement so that owners would be so relieved when he modified it they would accept neutering without much fuss. However, the Chap, who knows many leading politicians, says they are not that clever and never think that far ahead.

6 Ownership should carry legal responsibilities, as adoption does. These should include the canine right to adequate shelter in all weathers, regular food, and general care. The regulations should include the right of random inspection of all puppy farms, some of which break every rule of decent canine custom and see dogs only as pounds on paws.

7 The penalties for cruelty to dogs should be severe. Those convicted of particularly bad offences should be struck off the Register and banned from keeping dogs for a stated period or, in some instances, for life.

Some charity could even start a telephone Dogline to which those guilty of dog abuse could be reported in confidence.

8 There should be a Home Office code of practice governing the sale of dogs.

9 As a Community Social Service, social workers should be required to visit homes where puppies and

adult dogs have been rehoused to ensure that all is well. This is already happening in Essex and possibly elsewhere.

10 Owners should be required to keep their dogs healthy by means of the necessary inoculations and anti-parasite treatment.

11 No dogs should be allowed to roam freely out of human control. The turning out of dogs to exercise themselves should be illegal. Though some can look after themselves, looking right and left before crossing a road, the majority cannot. And any dog, like any human, can make a mistake or error of judgement. Allowing dogs to roam in the countryside also means that they are liable to hunt game or harry sheep, which may be fun but is likely to be life-shortening for the hunted and hunters alike.

12 All dogs should be entitled to adequate exercise on a daily basis so far as possible. When this is impracticable through owners' age or illness, social workers should arrange for neighbours or others to exercise them. It should be an offence to keep dogs chained up for long periods.

There should be freedom for all dogs that are under control to use the public parks and other open spaces. Why should we be banned because of the occasional tuppence? Would you ban yourself from walking in the countryside because of the occasional cowpat? If you can dodge a bovine tuppence you can dodge a canine one. To put it another way, if dogs are to be banned from public places because children might come into contact with their droppings, should town children be barred from the countryside because they might come into contact with the infected excreta of farm and wild animals?

In these violent days children in parks are much more likely to suffer harm from attack by horrible men than from dogs that are under control. Many older people would never go into parks if they did not have their dogs to exercise. Open spaces do not exist just for humans but for the birds and other creatures.

13 Dogs should be treated like other dependents, and owners should be encouraged to make arrangements for them in the event of their own demise. This could be done by ensuring that they will be cared for by relatives or friends, or leaving small legacies to ensure their financial support by some good professional kennel nominated in the will.

14 Many a poor dog is demoralized and bewildered when a marriage collapses. Some people have been known to stay together because neither could bear to be parted from the dog. There was even one old couple who wanted a divorce for many years, so incompatible had they become, but stayed together waiting for the dog to die. Sadly, however, such solicitude is rare, and too often the dog is sent to a home or becomes the cause of a fight over its custody. 'Tug of Labrador' was how a newspaper headlined such a bitter tussle recently. The rights of the dog do not seem to count for much in such cases, which provide further evidence of the extent to which we are at the mercy of human foibles. There is a glimmer of justice, however. A divorce court in Munich recently ordered a husband to pay substantial monthly alimony for two dogs and a cat.

While no home is complete without a dog, about half the homes in Britain fall into that category and I grieve for them. Still, there are about seven million of us in six million homes, some having two or more dogs, while in the USA the dog population is put at forty million. If only all the working dogs and show dogs could be encouraged to withdraw their labour while pet dogs – which I prefer to call companion dogs – withdrew their affection, what an impact we could make. Better still, picture the panic if we could all arise as one dog to enforce our rights! *'Allons chiens de la Patrie . . .'* What a stirring thought! It would be a formidable and frightening sight and those who were not with us would hold their doghoods cheap. Without doubt, we could also recruit thousands of human dog lovers to our cause. Anyone for *Canis*?

I am not campaigning on behalf of the Animal Rights in general and confess that the Rights of Cat leave me cold. The others will have to fight their own battles but to the Rights of Dog I am totally committed. So am I something of a revolutionary at heart? Not really. It would be nice to be a leader and spokesdog so that all the world would say, 'There is a dog!' but I am not intense enough by temperament for canine politics. All I am against, like so many of you, though not enough, is apathy in the struggle against injustice. Dogs' Rights are man's duties and if this book helps to stimulate more owners to action on our behalf then the year 2000 could open the century of the common dog. We might even secure a European Court of Canine Rights or, better still, a World Court, where those many countries that provide no legal protection to dogs and treat them all as curs could stand indicted in the name of common caninity.

All this may be just a bone dream but strange things are happening in the dog world these days. In 1990 a small town in California solemnly elected an eight-year-old Labrador-Rottweiler mongrel, called Bosco, as its mayor in preference to two human candidates. The townsfolk are reported as regarding His Honour, who wears his chain of office with dignity, as 'tough but fair'.

Sadly, there are parts of the world where dogs stand little or no chance of ever being emancipated. In Communist China, for instance, people who rear dogs are called 'decadent class enemies' and dogs that live on the street are clubbed to death. The dreadful plight of canine outlaws was brought home to me at a shoot where a man shied away from me because he loathes all dogs. He explained that he had lived for many years in Eastern and Middle Eastern countries where many dogs, called pariahs (a word first applied to human social outcasts in India), are condemned to be scavengers and get into such a terrible condition that he now cannot bear to have any dog near him. I submit that it is not the fault of the dogs.

Having got all that off my chest, I am now in a position to relate some of my adventures to date – the Adventures of a Chocolate Dog – for one dog in her time plays many parts.

16 Come Walk With Me

Hope springs eternal in the canine breast

Like a child, I can play alone with a toy, such as a ball, rubber bone or a stick, but, again like a child, I soon get bored with it. The need for someone to play with to expend excess energy is another relic from pack life that we are both saddled with. Both the Chap and the Boss romp with me, in the garden and the house, and it is a red-letter day when any grandchildren visit because they have more patience as well as more energy. On most days, however, when we are not fishing or shooting, my recreation is concentrated on walks, of which I always get at least three. With my thick coat and love of water I don't mind what the weather is like. The Chap's old ridgebacks, which hailed from hot, dry Africa, hated rain and believed that only mad dogs would go out in it but we Labradors are very much dogs for all seasons.

The first walk is to the post box which is eighty yards from our front door. Ridiculous though it may seem the Chap insists on taking me there, just in time to catch the 10 a.m. collection, saying that every yard counts. It is a bit of a joke in the village as we are seen going out and then back, all within five minutes, but I put my best paw forwards and get a few wall sniffs and a bark or two at other dogs. The Chap encourages me to encounter other dogs because for ninety-nine per cent of my life I do not live in a world of dogs. There is also the ever-delicious scent as we pass the butcher's shop and, on occasion, I am allowed to stare in wide-nostrilled wonder at the huge sides of beef being offloaded from the vans, what the Chap calls my 'Ah Bisto!' posture. Then we return along the path by the allotments where the Chap picks a few bits of fresh groundsel and chickweed for the canary.

Brief though the outing may be, I suppose the road-work also helps to keep my nails short so that I don't need to have them trimmed by the vet, which I would dislike.

I know that on most days that tiny trek has to last me until noon when I usually have to remind him that something more substantial is expected. We dogs have strong powers of anticipation and probably get more excited, internally, than any humans, including children, at the prospect of an adventure, which is what a walk always is for us. The tension begins when I sense that the clock must be reaching the point when we should be going out and mounts as I detect the signs that we are.

Usually by just sitting quietly and looking at him all the time, I manage to make my requirement plain and, eventually, my stare wears him down. The censure of a dog is something no man or woman can withstand. If he disappears into the loo with a book or his tape recorder I just curl up outside, often for a long and lonely vigil, so that he has to step over me when he opens the door. I suppose that in various ways I try to work on his conscience and I usually succeed.

He calls me a nagger though I am trying to get him out for his own good, a reason which, he says, has been the cry of the nagger down the ages. The females of the human species have a reputation for nagging and I try not to nag him too much but there are times when he wears out my patience. His stock answer when I try to prise him away from his word processor – 'I have to work to earn the dog food' – makes me suspect that he loves the machine more than he loves me (and his wife thinks the same about herself). The trouble is that he has always 'just got to do this' or 'just got to do that' and I have learned that 'Wait a minute' can mean quite a long time. In fact he deserves to be called Mr Just, and not because he is particularly even-handed.

When I have won I know that we are going on a longish walk as soon as he picks up his blackthorn thumbstick – his third leg, as he calls it, which is very useful, especially when there is ice on the road. I can also tell where we are going from which dog lead he takes. If he takes the short lead with a little spike on one end I know that we are going to the river and I jump into the car. If he takes the extensible lead – a cord wound in a spring-loaded coil, I know we are going for a local walk. The long lead is better because I can pull it out about ten yards and that increases my sniffing range but I don't like it when the line gets round my tail and parts adjacent to it.

I am not supposed to pull on the lead and when I do the Chap keeps saying, 'Heel! Heel!' but when we are going up hill he encourages me to pull, shouting, 'Mush! Mush!' whatever that may mean. I am quite happy to give the old boy a helping paw but it would make life easier if he stuck to one command.

We always start off through the churchyard which is only a few yards from our front door. The twelfth-century church has lots of trees and old tombs and gravestones going back centuries. There is a story that one of the tombs contains a sword buried with a soldier and that it can sometimes be heard rattling in the darkness. I have been in the churchyard at midnight and never heard a thing. Not even an owl.

The number of gravestones, some of which date back to the sixteenth century, is getting smaller, now that nobody else is being buried there. Village yobbos push them over and once they are broken they tend to be set on one side and forgotten. Odd, isn't it, that yob is boy spelled backwards? Perhaps they are backward boys. Anyway, they have no respect for the dead but, come to that, neither have I.

Of course there are no dog graves because dogs, however precious to their owners, cannot be buried on consecrated ground. Some old churches had special pews for the squire's dogs but dogs are not allowed in our church. I am an exception because the lady verger, Elsie, is a friend of mine and she let me in one hot summer's day when it was wonderfully cool inside. She said that there used to be an annual service for pets and is trying to resurrect it. I noticed that the vicar wears his dog collar for a service but not very often outside, as the Chap says they always used to when he was a boy.

Our church is well known for its peal of bells which, being so close, we hear rather well, though they are not too loud. The bells summon the faithful but very few come, except for weddings, christenings and funerals. When a dog lover dies it tolls for me.

At each end of the churchyard there is a notice about the need for dogs to be kept on a lead, any one which fouls the area being *'canis non grata'*. There is no way I would do such a thing. I always try to get out of sight if I can when answering Nature's most urgent call. It may look like modesty but we dogs have no hang-ups about our natural functions or fallacies about the body being vile. It is, in fact, another inheritance from my wolf ancestry. For those few awkward moments, when I agree that we look rather ridiculous, we are very vulnerable to attack.

Spending tuppence, as the Chap calls it, is far less disgusting than the human trademark – the litter on the pavements, the roads, the lanes, the lay-bys, anywhere. There is a seat in the churchyard which is heavily used by visitors and young villagers who throw all their beer cans, cigarette packets and plastic food containers around, though there is a litter bin handy. There is no notice up about their behaviour though their offence now carries a much bigger fine than a dog's would. In Dover, such litter-louts are being publicly shamed by a yellow Labrador, called Shelley, which has been trained to pick up everything from empty drinks cans to fast-food cartons and cigarette packets and to drop them all into litter bins along the seafront. It is a splendid example which I might follow, one day.

There is now a movement for dog walkers to carry what is called a 'poop-scoop' to remove any dogure and take it home. Logically, it should follow that parents should be required to accompany their children with a bag or bin and to pick up all the crisp bags, ice-cream containers, toffee papers, drink cans and other litter with which they so gaily festoon the streets, parks and countryside.

The trouble is that, with your heads so high in the air and your minds on less important matters, you don't really look where you are going. I never tread in any dogure and with four legs I have twice as big a chance as you of doing so. All this fuss about dogs fouling pavements and paths seems so trivial to us compared with the scale of what you are doing. The raw sewage from millions of your big bodies goes into the rivers and seas every day. Even the smell of dog excrement is nothing compared with the smell of sewage farms. The stench from one of them as we approach Windsor on the M4 is quite appalling at all times and I can't believe that there are no germs in it. How the Queen puts up with this tribute from her loyal subjects when the wind is in the wrong direction I do not know, though I suppose that the Windsor Castle residents contribute to it. It is a disgusting process of polluting the air which people breathe and is widespread throughout the country, even on our little Common. If dogs were responsible for the smell there would be national outrage.

What you call spending a penny but which costs me only the effort doesn't count as fouling in the churchyard. I'm in debt to plants for oxygen so I repay them with nitrogen, wherever I happen to be. At least, that's how I look at it. I'm sure that it helps to make the snowdrops grow.

While on that subject I will explain why we seem to be so choosy about exactly where the penny should be spent, a habit which sometimes fusses you when you are in a hurry. A dog is so made that it needs to be triggered off by a scent stimulus, so we have to search around until we find it. It is no good trying to hurry us up. We have to find the right place before it can happen. Always remember that there are plenty of places where you wouldn't do it!

Just after we have gone through the gate into the churchyard we pass the war memorial to the village dead of two world wars. There are scores of names carved on the stem of the granite cross, though in those days this was a tiny village so it is a far more eloquent memorial to man's inhumanity to man. It is one of the best places for catching the Chap off guard by wrapping the long lead round it, especially if he happens to stop there to pass the time of day with some other villager. As he tries to catch up with me to unravel it I simply go on round and round. My best to date is three turns but I have managed four round a lime tree a little further on.

After leaving the churchyard we go down a sloping path and I meet my first dog, an elderly black Labrador at the Old Vicarage. He never fails to bark however much I try to make friends with him but he's only defending his territory. I am always chary about the next bit because it is across a narrow bridge over the Kennet-Avon canal and I might face the situation I like least – a strange dog in front of me and one coming behind at the same time. Like any good general I don't fancy having to defend myself on two fronts for, in the dog world, discretion is usually the better part of valour and one needs a line of retreat. When I might have to brave the situation I just steel myself and say, 'Be a dog!' though I know that the Chap wouldn't let me come to much harm, armed as he is with his thumbstick.

If the coast is clear I am tall enough – almost four feet standing on my hind legs – to get my head over the parapet and see what ducks and coots are available for spooking on the canal. As the Chap says, time spent on reconnaissance is rarely wasted.

Once over the bridge we have a choice of two walks. We can go straight on down a leafy lane, called the Avenue, or we can turn down on to the towpath of the Kennet-Avon canal. There is no traffic either way so I can run free. Each way offers the comfortable pleasure of a familiar route. You should never think that we are likely to be bored on a walk we know well. Variety is fun but familiarity is the spice of our life. The familiar route makes us feel safe and at ease. New smells are interesting but on a familiar route I can sniff the plants and branches and make a mental inventory of what has happened since I was last there, especially as regards visits by male dogs, which interest me most.

As we females always squat to mark, once we have found a suitable place, we can leave scent only on the ground. By cocking their legs the males can leave

161

it high upon walls and branches. So a high mark automatically tells me that it was made by a male dog, though I can identify it by the scent, too. To assert its authority, each dog tries to mark higher than the last and some are very good at it. Of course the bigger dogs have a built-in advantage – you would hardly expect a Yorkshire Terrier to compete with an Alsatian – but agility and pressure also count and some small ones do very well. Aim is also important. At one shoot, which the Chap used to attend regularly, there was a black Labrador which had extraordinary aim. He would sidle up to whoever happened to be wearing rubber boots and direct a stream right inside one of them, the hot trickle being the first sign that the garrulous wearer knew of it. The Chap says that this Labrador was the finest canine shot he has ever seen and was never off form.

The way the dogs can ration their marks to a few drops at a time is due to a special mechanism denied to humans. We females can do it to some extent, especially when we are in season. I have to say that it is the really high marks that interest me most and I spend a long time savouring them. I suppose that I am reading with my nose.

Sometimes I am allowed to choose the route and I always prefer the towpath. Then I am by the water all the way and there's always something going on there. Fortunately the Chap often prefers it because there are plenty of plantains there which he picks for my friend George, the canary, who loves them, and always gives us his special 'Thank you' squawk when he gets one on our return.

The Chap doesn't like walking for the sake of it. A walk must have a purpose. He uses it to extend his knowledge of the wild flowers, butterflies and birds and enjoys looking at the coarse fish, like the roach, carp, perch and bream, but most of the time is spent thinking about his next book or article. On all our walks, and even when fishing on the river, he is forever talking into his pocket tape recorder with ideas and instructions to himself. Much of the time when he talks to me he is really talking aloud to himself. When anybody ribs him about it he falls back on the story about St Francis who talked to birds and was made a saint. Rum, isn't it? But nothing about human behaviour surprises me.

Though we call our treks 'walks' I do like to get on at my natural loping pace – a dog-trot in which the back legs propel my body while the front legs support and guide. To conform with your life we have to be inactive most of our time so we do like to get on with the action when we can. Our endurance is so superior to yours that I could travel 75 miles in a day, as a gun dog often does out hunting, and still be ready for more. Humans use a phrase 'dog-tired' but I am still full of energy and ready for any action when my Chap staggers up to bed exhausted. 'Man-tired' would be a more honest term.

Sometimes when my couple are watching athletics on TV the victors are lauded to the sky, yet, by arching my back at a gallop to extend the spread of my stride, I could beat the lot of them at almost all the track and endurance events. And I would do it without the benefit of dope. Further, it would be accomplished so much more gracefully on four legs. We accelerate so much more quickly than you two-legged creatures, which is why sprinters start on four limbs. And with four-leg brakes we can come to a stop more abruptly without overbalancing. We can also turn more easily. Physically we are superior in so many ways.

By the canal I have great fun with the water voles. I freeze as soon as one is in smell, just like a wolf does, stalk it with the patience of a spider and then pounce, jumping high into the air, to try to catch it with my forepaws. I have never caught one yet because they always have an escape route into the water but their luck will run out one day. Dabchicks are also exciting. I love to see them jump into the water and then paddle away leaving a trail of bubbles. And of course the mallards, which are half-tame on the canal, are always good for a quick charge to drive them into the water. In the late summer the drakes moult and look like ducks. I don't quite do that but in summer, owing to the action of sunlight, my fur undergoes a colour change and my ears and head look more like milk chocolate, which means a lighter shade of grey to me. There are also a few swans on the canal but I don't tangle with them, pretending that I haven't heard their hisses.

On rare occasions we scent a dog-fox's mark. I say 'we' because even the Chap can detect and identify that, it is so overpowering.

Because there are so many nettles along the towpath the place is rich in butterflies and, though I chase them, I have never caught one. I have caught the nettles though, more than once, and right on the nose. It was unpleasant and my Chap's effort to relieve the sting by rubbing my nose with a dock leaf just didn't work. Old wives' tales don't work for bitches. I have also been stung on the nose by a wasp. The Chap said it was a near squeak because a wasp sting inside the mouth can be fatal if the tongue swells up. The Chap tries to stop me snapping at them when they buzz round me in the garden but I'm afraid I can't resist it. 'Some dogs never learn,' he mutters when I snap at one of the pests. But I can prove that I do. Occasionally on the tow-path there is a gaily coloured, horse-drawn narrow boat and sometimes we meet the horse and I always give it a wide berth. I was once kicked by a horse and still have a scar on one of my back legs, though unlike humans I do not draw attention to my operation.

Since the Queen opened the canal in 1990 there are many more narrow boats and cabin cruisers and the crews usually give us a cheery wave, even sometimes asking what kind of a dog I am when they don't happen to have seen a chocolate Labrador before. There was great excitement when the Chap spotted a boat called Dido, though apparently it was no new thing because the Royal Navy has had at least two warships with that famous name.

To ring the changes, the Chap took me on the horse-drawn narrow boat, all the way from Kintbury to Hungerford. The other passengers made a fuss of me and I was able to bark at a few dogs on the towpath but it is really more fun to run than to cruise.

The canal boats are not popular with the anglers who pursue the so-called coarse fish and are an extra interest for us both. The Chap started his angling life in the North as a maggot fisher and while most people would regard him as very odd, if not crackpot, when he asks some fisherman if he can smell his tin of squirming maggots it makes good sense to me. The unmistakable smell reminds him of the magic of the days when he started fishing as a boy, showing that, for a few things anyway, he has strong scent memories like I have.

The only things I dislike about these fishermen are the huge green umbrellas under which they shelter from the rain and wind. You can never be sure who or what is lurking behind them so I am in the habit of giving them a good bark, which is not always well received, especially if the character within happens to be snoozing. Most of the anglers have such a collection of rods, reels, nets, floats and trays of bait, that they seem afraid that I will do some damage if I nose around them. As some of the very long rods, called roach-poles, can cost about £1,000 the Chap makes sure that I am under control. The anglers, too, are quick to take action when they see me coming, scrabbling up their maggots as though they were gold which, at five pounds a tin, they are.

The alternative route to the Canal Turn, called the Avenue, is a narrow half-mile drive to an old mansion and was built for the owners to be able to drive their carriages to the church in privacy and shade. To me it seems to have been made for dogs. There are dog-roses and dog violets, the word 'dog' suggesting that they are somehow inferior to the real thing, though the dog rose is one of the main species from which all the garden roses sprang. There are also dog's mercury, dog's-tail grass, and dog's-tongue. My Chap has even tried to plant dogwood in what he calls his secret memorial garden to three of his old dogs who used to accompany him on his walks there. He also put in a lot of effort in the spring planting marguerites, cornflowers and columbine but most of them died because they could not compete with the wild weeds, just as I couldn't compete with a wolf in the wild. The pampering of cultivation makes everything soft and you and I are no exceptions. A few of the Chap's transplants survived, however, and I see that he is trying to plant up the memorial garden again in the autumn when the weeds are dying down. The old fellow is nothing if not persistent. If he succeeds it won't do much for me, though. All flowers look grey to my eyes.

There are several bridges along the Avenue and the first, which is over the railway, has solid metal sides which the local yobbos adorn with graffiti, however often these are painted out at considerable expense by the railway company. This strange human habit goes so far back in history – there are graffiti in Westminster Abbey, in old castles and even archaeological sites – that I wonder if it really started with creatures like us. If you think about it, what the scribblers are doing is leaving their mark for others to see, just as we leave marks for other dogs to smell. Indeed, a lot of the statements have a sexual content. So the side of the bridge is a kind of human scenting post. 'Kilroy was here'. The big difference is that while human graffiti are destructive and cost money to remove, ours are quickly gone with the wind and rain.

When I have spent a penny or tuppence on grass or earth, but not on sharp stones, I scrape the ground vigorously with my paws, all four of them, to leave still more scent from my pads and so intensify my personal stamp. My Chap calls it my 'Muhammad Ali shuffle' because some boxer, who also happened to be chocolate coloured, used to make a similar motion in the ring for fun. In the process, I also leave scratch marks in the soft earth as a visual mark. Wolves do the same so I wonder if man's primitive ancestors started leaving scratch marks that way. Was that the origin of art? Are those paintings in caves, which show dogs, among other creatures, a form of graffiti? Just a suggestion!

Further along the Avenue there is a beautiful river bridge built by Napoleonic prisoners of war. It needed repair and, before that could be done, village louts pushed one whole side of it into the river. We may tear up the odd slipper or book when we are young and frustrated but we are never so destructive on such a scale. Vandals seem to have so little reason in their heads that it is overcome by one can of beer. Having little hope of ever creating anything, all they can do is destroy. My friend, Colin, the builder who lives opposite to us, rebuilt the bridge out of the goodness of his heart but it has not been possible to recover some of the ancient bricks from the water. I am pleased it has been repaired because we make a lot of new friends by it in the spring and summer, the trout fly-fishermen who all make a fuss of me.

Another of our regular walks is on the Common, about two miles away, where I can run where I like and show my tracking skill. If my Chap hides in the bushes, as he sometimes does, I can track him down though there are scores of other human tracks criss-crossing his. To my nose his recent scent is like a newly painted signpost would be to your eyes. I never fail to dog his footsteps but he could never man my paw-steps.

For half the year there is a large herd of cattle on the Common and occasionally, until I am stopped, I sidle up on these pack animals in the manner in which I expect wolves do on grazing caribou. They know it's only a game, though, and usually I end up nose-to-nose with one of them. I cannot speak their language but somehow we communicate and they take it in good humour.

What I admire about the cattle is their determination to enforce their right of way on the roads crossing the Common and make all the cars, and the humans in them, wait on their pleasure. When we are held up by them they give us a contemptuous 'We were here first' look, which is always a telling argument, or should be. Sometimes I am encouraged to gyp them up with a bark from the car if we are going into the little local town of Hungerford and I enjoy that too.

As with all herbivorous animals, the gases escaping from the bodies of the cattle help to deplete the ozone layer to such an extent worldwide that it is supposed to be partly responsible for the greenhouse effect. I fear that, on occasion, I must do the ozone layer a bit of no good myself. But what we do to our joint environment is as nothing compared with your depredations.

17 Arms and the Dog

Every dog in arms should wish to be.

For most of his adult life, the Chap has been a keen gameshot. While showing concern for a tom-tit that has stunned itself by flying into the window, he enjoys knocking down high-flying pheasants. He has, therefore, always owned gun dogs in the shape of springer spaniels. At his old house, which was remote, he used to shoot rabbits out of the bedroom window at five in the morning, filling the bedroom with fumes, and his dogs would run out and retrieve them. Happily he can't do that here. The neighbours would object and, anyway, there are no rabbits in our walled garden.

Naturally, he hoped that, in addition to my other qualities, I would fulfil that purpose. It wasn't part of the deal, and he knows that, but it would have been a nice bonus. Sadly for him, I had not been trained to retrieve game when I was young and, as everyone conveniently believes, it is not easy to teach old dogs new tricks. (In fact, this myth probably originated from the behaviour of smart dogs who did not want to learn how to work and that includes me.)

Fetching and carrying are pawual and jawual tasks and I'm an intellectual, agreeing with the Chap that I have as much right to that description as some of the men and women who claim it. Further, having heard how the Chap takes it out on his word processor when things go wrong what might he say to me if I misbehaved and made him look foolish at some posh shoot? I have heard him tell of an Earl who was never asked again to a famous shoot because he had laughed when a Labrador, which wasn't even his, got into a big drive and spooked the pheasants. If shooters are that touchy what mayhem might I cause?

At this stage it might be instructive to ask why humans indulge in organized sport like game-shooting, where several men pit their wits and skill against a challenging situation? Surely the answer is sticking out like a sore paw – it is the re-enactment of the pack in pursuit of quarry. This, I would wager, is the elemental basis of all team games like football, rugby, hockey and cricket. They rekindle the primitive pleasure men derived from hunting together in a pack. With team games it is fitting that the ball is usually made from an animal's hide.

Considering our long association in the hunt for game, which has come to mean creatures killed for pleasure, it is proper that there should be dogs at shoots and, in many ways, I would like to be one of them. When I was still a pup I was taken beating on a pheasant shoot and I loved sniffing the birds out and then seeing them fly. With a nose like mine I have no problem in finding living creatures trying to hide themselves and I instinctively point at them with one leg up. So what I would like to do on shoots is to hunt and Labradors which are trained to retrieve are not usually allowed to do that. Making live birds fly is my game. Picking up corpses in my mouth is simply not my cup of milk.

I also discovered that dogs-at-arms are treated as servants and usually live outside in servants' quarters called kennels and I did not fancy that at all.

Except when they are out shooting, perhaps once or twice a week, they are yard dogs. This means that, while they may have quarters which are good to look at, with what is called a 'nice' run, they are isolated away from the pack for most of their lives. If they are only dogs, as most gun dogs are, then they live cruelly lonely lives by my reckoning, spending most of their time looking out wistfully for human company. However nice a run a dog may have, it does not run on it much if it is on its own, any more than a child would. It just sits disconsolately.

Most professional dog handlers believe that the warmth of a house is bad for a dog because it is 'unnatural' but the pleasure of a fireside is something we have shared with you for centuries, probably since we were both cave dwellers together. If it is 'unnatural' for us after all this time so it is for you. Even the dedicated athlete does not think that sitting in front of a fire in the evening is going to make him soft, provided he does not do too much of it. It won't make us soft either, if we get sufficient exercise. Since our body temperature is higher than yours it could be argued that we need artificial heat more than you do.

Gun dogs themselves also tend to be professionals and an amateur like I would be could make herself look silly competing with them. I am not ambitious to excel either in the field or in the show-ring. I suppose that some dogs must be, like racehorses seem to try to win for the joy of it. In my view, though, it does not pay, in the human environment, to appear to be too clever – or too obliging. As has been said of humans, the height of cleverness is to be able to conceal it. I have heard it said that monkeys can really talk but never do because they know that if they did they would be given work to do. Anyway, I am too well pleased with my lot to want to be an ordinary career dog, though a literary career is a different matter.

On the second day of our association the Chap tried me out with a rubber bone. I ran and picked it up when he shouted, 'Fetch it!' but did not return it to him. Why should I? I want him to chase me. That's the game I like. He looked rather disappointed. His spaniels had always obliged.

One of his books suggested that after throwing the object he should crouch down on one knee to get himself to my level, and then open his arms wide and make pleading noises. I was so fascinated by this performance that all I could do was stare at him in amazement. It looked more like a proposal of marriage than a retrieving exercise.

The book advised him against persisting with any method that did not work and to try something new. As I am such a water dog his next move was to try to 'break me in' – what an aggressive term – with a stick thrown into the water. I went after that as soon as he shouted, 'Fetch it!' because I love a swim and I always brought it back and dropped it fairly close to him but I would not deliver it to his hand. Anyway, he thought he was making progress and threw the stick on dry land. I was not interested in it because there was no swimming. Again, he looked sadly disappointed.

In our parts, dead pheasants for training practice are easy to come by at any time of the year. There are so many around us that some are killed on the roads almost every day by drivers who, literally, do not give a hoot about wildlife. The Chap's reaction is an interesting commentary on the human mind. He hoots the horn wildly if he sees a pheasant on the road to frighten it to safety, holding up the traffic in the process. He enjoys killing a high pheasant with his gun but when he sees one which has been killed by a car he invariably murmurs, 'What a shame! What a waste!' I suspect that when he stops to pick one up that is not too mutilated, other drivers think he is scavenging for the pot but it is really to try out my retrieving capability, or lack of it, yet again. It's an ill tragedy that does nobody some good. (I think I have said something quite profound there, if you think about it.)

He first tested me in the garden by throwing a small dead pheasant. I ran to it all right but there was no way that I was going to pick it up. Having no sense of duty, which is a purely human phenomenon, we do things for you because we enjoy it and I don't enjoy feathers. I just sat with it and the look on the Chap's face was a mixture of puzzlement and dismay. There was sound reason behind my apparent ineptitude. When I was out beating, while I was young, I picked up a pigeon which had been shot and got a mouth full of horrible dry feathers. The psychologists are always trying to find some seminal event which happened in childhood and got repressed. I reckon that picking up that pigeon was mine.

He fooled me by smuggling a dead pheasant down to the river in a plastic bag under his jacket and throwing the bird upstream into the water. I swam out, grabbed it, thinking it was a feathery stick, and brought it back close to the side because as the feathers were wet they did not fill my mouth with fluff. On the second throw, however, I got rid of it in midstream and away went the bird over the weir.

Further, my reason tells me that if I am going to find a tasty bird I should be able to eat it. After all, that's why the humans want it. But that is definitely disallowed for dogs.

The Chap then tried striding ahead of me when we were out for a walk and dropping his handkerchief in the hope that I would sense that he had lost it and would pick it up and take it to him. He did this because his last springer spaniel, Skipper, would do it every time on his own initiative. Of course I saw

the handkerchief but assumed, as any really intelligent dog would, having seen him deliberately drop
it, that he had thrown it away. When he tried to
order me back to fetch it I thought, 'I'll be man-gone
if I will,' not when he'd dropped it deliberately. So
that ploy did not work either.

Realizing that he had a tough job on his hands the
Chap thought that, before wasting any more of his
precious time, he had better find out if I was gun-shy
– frightened of the sound of a shotgun going off at
close quarters – because that would bar me from the
shooting field. So off we went to the local gun school,
accompanied by his eleven-year-old grandson, Daniel,
who was learning to shoot. Of course I wasn't gun-shy,
though I did not have the benefit of earmuffs which the
others wore. I am shy of nothing. All I wanted to do
was to go after the clay pigeons which were missed.
The Chap had once owned a springer spaniel, called
Honey, which would retrieve clay pigeons provided
they were still perfect but would never bring back a
broken one. But I was not allowed to show whether I
could do that. I doubt that I would have brought one
back. I was shown one later. It was round, black, ined-
ible, smelt of bitumen and was generally uninteresting.

I did not learn much at the gun school but it was
illuminating to see Daniel hit the first three clay pigeons
with his 28-bore gun and then watch the Chap miss
four with his 12-bore – a blunderbuss by comparison.
Perhaps that was a clue to what was in his mind.
People who are not very good shots are more likely
to be invited to shoots if they have a good gun dog.

'She's not gun-shy – just work-shy,' I heard him
say to the Boss on our return. He could have a point,
nevertheless he could hardly wait to continue with his
hopeless task. For his next trick he tried a different tack.
Having discovered that I like chocolate drops he got the
idea of hiding them and saying, 'Fetch it,' in the hope

that it would encourage me to use my sense of smell and seek things out. Every evening he and the Boss hid about a dozen chocolate drops in various parts of the living room and then let me in to find them. I hoovered around until I had them all. I cannot count much above four – no dog can – but I never missed one. I think it made me use my nose a bit more but it got him no nearer making me any more interested in retrieving a bird, though hopefully he will go on trying – with an on-going supply of dog-chocs.

As I will be describing in more detail, I am very interested indeed in fishing and fish. I get excited when the Chap hooks one and am keen to see and examine it when it is landed. This gave the Chap the idea that he might get somewhere by teaching me to retrieve a dead fish and bring it to him but I fear that the experiments were another failure. I am not interested in being a fish-porter, even if my Newfoundland ancestors were.

He decided to take me to a few shoots to watch the other dogs in the hope that I might copy them, but so far in the trial of wills I have won and the Chap seems to know when he's beaten. Doesn't that suggest a higher intelligence than the dog that is only too willing to oblige? At least I have demonstrated that while I obey on most things I am not a slave. I have heard it said that there are three kinds of gun dogs – gentlemen's dogs, keepers' dogs and beaters' dogs. In fact there is a fourth kind. I am my own dog!

However, whenever I sense a pheasant on our walks and put it up, as I often do, it seems to rekindle the Chap's determination because it irritates him that I have such a good nose for a game bird (as he says he had himself when he was younger, though I don't know quite what he means.) Sometimes, still living in the hope that I might be a late developer, he hides a dead pheasant in the garden when I am not looking and then sends me for it. I always find it and manage to dog-handle it out of the bushes but I don't fancy picking it up. I suppose that I have got everything it takes to be a good gun dog except the will.

The other day he was discussing a monstrous new device called an electronic collar which delivers an electric shock when the handler presses a button after a dog in training has not performed exactly as it should. Dog alive! I've never heard of such a barbaric imposition. The idea is that the dog does not associate the shock with the handler but only with the failure to oblige him. I reckon that this dog would have no trouble at all in realizing who was responsible.

I don't feel too badly about my uncooperative behaviour because he has really given up the pretence of serious shooting, being on the verge of giving it up altogether. He has even got to the stage of wearing a joke badge when he has shot badly at a drive with friends. It reads, 'Over the hill,' and saves a lot of excuses. All he really wants now is a pal at his peg – the numbered place where he stands at each drive – and I am more than happy to be a peg-dog and to sympathize with him when he is off form. If that isn't enough I know I'll regret it when he goes shooting without me but maybe he'll take me for the ride or the Boss will take me along in the afternoon, when, I gather, she usually goes. On the other hand if I become famous he might find he is invited because of me and then I shall have to be taken.

Meanwhile there is a continuing battle of wills which, at the moment I am determined to win. If I happen to be in a mischievous mood, though, I may surprise him one day, and myself in the process, by retrieving a pheasant. One of his shooting friends had a peke which could not retrieve but was always taken along because she would find a bird and sit on it until her master came to pick it up. Maybe I could do that, though I don't think I would have the patience to do it for long.

In the meantime, what I really like is fishing. Perhaps, in my heart of hearts, I disapprove of other blood sports. Pheasants and partridges are much more interesting to me when they can run and fly.

18 Call to Arms

'Shooting is a dogly sport.'

In spite of my reluctance the Chap could not resist the first opportunity to take me partridge shooting though I had only just finished my heat. We could hardly be said to have got off to a good start. To avoid any diversions of attention by other dogs he sprayed me with some stuff called Anti-Mate which smelled like lemons, which I don't like. As we were getting out of our car, one of the other shooters remarked, 'Dear God, is that stink you or your dog?'

By letting me out well before we reached the home of our shooting host, the Chap had already ensured that I would not disgrace us by spending tuppence on the lawn. But as soon as we got to the parking place for the first drive I needed to repeat the process. It was not my fault that the host and hostess should stop their vehicle just by my offering and exactly where the lady would have to alight.

Taking no chances when we got to our first stand, the Chap produced the enormous corkscrew goat-tether with which he had threatened me for so long and screwed it into the soft ground. So I was well anchored. I think that I was the only dog that was pegged down. The others just sat, obediently, in front of their owners showing little interest even when a hare came out. I suppose that it was as well that I was pegged because I do not think I would have been able to resist running after the hare. As it was, I could not avoid a little bark which produced black looks from all. On the whole, though, I was as good as Pedigree Chum.

Not many partridges came over us but scores of pheasants did. The pheasants were in season but they were not shot because they were all too low and too easy and some were too young. It seems stupid to me that they shoot only at the difficult ones. In the wild we would always catch the easy ones, especially young ones, which are more tasty. The whole attitude of the shooters to the game seemed odd – a kind of love-kill relationship. They like and admire the birds, spending a fortune to rear and feed them, then delight in killing far more than they can possibly eat. When a pheasant is put up by the beaters they say, 'Up goes £15' (the cost of rearing it), 'bang goes 10p' (the cost of a cartridge), and 'down comes 75p' (the value of the bird on the market). Not very sensible economics is it?

When the drive was over the Chap released me from the corkscrew but then attached the extensible lead and took me looking for a couple of partridges which he had managed to shoot. I found them easily but I didn't pick them up. Among the other shooters, who all had trained dogs, there was much blowing of whistles, some of them of the kind that humans can't hear, much calling of names and much praise and blame when birds were brought back or missed. The dogs would probably have performed better if they had been allowed to do it their way instead of being given so much back-seat advice. I even heard one man apologize to his dog for failing to provide enough partridges to pick up, with a promise to do better. It seemed to me that some of the dogs, as well as the shooters, were prone to exhibitionism.

After the next drive, the Chap took me to watch another special dog, a Field Trials Champion finding, picking up and returning the birds to its owners. His ploy was to see whether jealousy would do the trick and I would copy it. It didn't, not even when the dog was sent to pick up one of our partridges. It didn't work because I did not regard the birds as my property. I wasn't jealous at all, not even when he made a fuss of the other dog in front of me, being only too happy to see someone else make all the effort.

Actually there wasn't really much work to do because there were lots of professional pickers-up, men and women paid to do the job and anxious to show their skills. The few birds retrieved by the shooters' dog could easily have been picked up by hand. It seems to be the same at all the shoots the Chap attends so why he is so anxious for me to retrieve I cannot understand. Having a useful dog seems to be just part of the ritual with which big-time shooting is heavily endowed. For instance, the wives and girl friends all turn up in shooting gear though they never shoot. Some only appear at lunch but still arrive in shooting togs with large hats adorned with feathers. I can only think that they regard a shooting day as a little fashion parade.

After the first drive in the afternoon, one of the shooters, a rather peppery gentleman, asked the Chap, 'What's the point of bringing a dog that can't pick up?'

With no trace of a smile, the Chap replied, 'She's here in a different professional capacity.'

'What the hell's that?'

'She's collecting material for a book she's writing. Be careful what you say in front of her because you might be in it.'

The look on the man's face indicated that he doubted the Chap's sanity and he kept well away from us for the rest of the afternoon.

I noticed that all the shooters tried to keep a smiling face even when they had not shot well or had drawn bad positions in the line which gave them little to shoot at. The Chap wasn't very good at doing that. When he is miserable he looks it.

The day taught me that some shooters are quite fanatical about their sport and seem to think of little else. When one of them, who had a stomach upset, needed to go to the loo in the bushes and returned without success he said that he had had a blank drive! I heard only one wise remark, in a drinks-time discussion about whether gun dogs should be kept in the house – 'You can't spoil a good dog', with which I thoroughly agree. When we got back home the Boss asked, expectantly, 'How did she get on?'

'She lived up to her name,' the Chap replied, glumly.

'Meaning what?'

'Did naught.'

It took a moment or two for the Boss to realize that he meant Did O, meaning Zero. But if it comes to making fun of names the Chap starts on a sticky wicket.

About a fortnight later we went to a duck shoot, where the Chap had higher hopes because of my natural love of water. A lot of the dead ducks fell into a lake and I needed little encouragement to plunge in. I picked up a duck in my mouth and swam to the shore with it but seeing some others I dropped it and the Chap nearly fell in trying to bring it closer with his thumbstick. He seemed to rate my efforts at bringing several close to the bank as a major step forward. In fact he was so excited that I thought I would make his day and actually brought in a duck, climbed on the bank with it and delivered it to his hand. The jubilation by the Chap and the Boss was so great that one would have thought that they had won the Pools. The others, whose dogs were bringing ducks out by the dozen, must have thought them slightly mad to be making such a fuss.

Of course, he immediately set me after another duck, hoping that I would repeat the process, having received so much praise, but, having proved to one and all that I could do it, what was the point of proving it again? Too much success at once might go to his head. He's already vain enough.

We then went on to the pheasants where the Chap shot a high bird which fell so far behind us that one of the professional pickers sent off one of his black Labradors to retrieve it. Instead of doing that, the dog came right to our peg, inspected the Chap's leather gun-sleeve and spent a penny on it. While he was chasing the dog off, in fury, the dog-man released his other Labrador to retrieve the dead pheasant. For some reason this dog was also more interested in the gun-sleeve and spent tuppence on it. Everyone else hooted but the Chap was not amused because we were stuck with the smell in the car for the rest of the day.

In the afternoon I found a half-eaten pheasant, left from a previous shoot, and picked it up, thinking I might be allowed to eat it. Instead the Chap took it from me with almost a whoop of delight 'She's brought me half a pheasant! We are half way there!'

A little later I nearly brought him another half when I had a tug-of-war with a Labrador which was taking a shot bird to its master. I think I was winning until the Chap hastily pulled me away with copious apologies all round.

My greatest excitement came when we were standing on the edge of a wood and a fox appeared – perhaps the fox which had half eaten that pheasant. I had never seen one before and the smell was terrific. My Chap won't shoot a fox because it looks too much like a dog, which is very touching I think. He says that foxes seem to know this because they always come out where he is standing. Usually, shoot owners want them shot because they kill so much game, so he pretends not to see them and to be deaf when everyone is shouting 'Tally Ho!' or 'Charlie!', which is another name for a fox. He won't shoot anything big, not even a hare.

Later, when he summoned up the courage to release me, I caused quite a scare by running off to the edge of the wood, where I had seen a pheasant poke its head out. The Chap thought I might go inside but he doesn't realize that I don't like getting out of sight of him. 'Out of sight out of mind' is a good motto for a dog and I do my best to be in his mind all the time.

As had happened at the partridge shoot, all we got to take home was two birds though the Chap had probably shot about forty. The rest went to market. It didn't seem much reward to me for so much effort but all the shooters seemed well pleased and convinced themselves that it had been a wonderful day though we had all been drenched.

Even though I still had not retrieved another bird to hand, the Chap remained hopeful enough to take me to shoots, including famous ones, like Highclere and Broadlands, where I suppose I should feel very honoured to be standing, or rather sitting, in the line along with Lords and Admirals of the Fleet. At Broadlands the Chap and I experienced the ultimate in open-air living – after the first stand one of the shooters sent his driver-butler round with vintage champagne and a tray bearing hard-boiled eggs cut in half and a large tin of the best caviare! I got a tiny bit which must surely be the first time that a dog has been fed caviare at a shoot.

At the last shoot I was so much admired by a dog-trainer for my looks and ability to find game that he guaranteed to teach me to retrieve if he could take me away for four months. The Chap was not tempted for a moment, saying that he could not possibly be separated from me for such a long time. Actually, at the end of the day, he had decided that I could never be any good because I had whined so much when the pheasants started falling that he had assured the owner that it would be 'Dido's Last Stand'.

Nevertheless, while I have probably said my farewell to arms, he still perseveres in trying to make me into a gun dog, using various gambits to try to stop me whining. There is one last resort which was used with occasional success by a friend of his who had an equally vocal Labrador called Piggy. This man carried a soda siphon in a haversack partly to dilute his occasional Scotch but mainly to squirt at Piggy when she whined. The Chap hasn't tried this yet but, knowing his penchant for experiment, he probably will if he becomes desperate.

Why does he go on trying to make me into a sporting bitch? It could be that he refuses to be beaten when, as everybody says, I look the part so well when I am sitting quietly at the peg before the birds begin to fly. Or perhaps, in his long life, he has met so many females who kept saying 'No' but eventually obliged. His patient efforts have put me in a bit of a dilemma. I would like to keep him shooting for a few more seasons, because that would be beneficial for the health of both of us. The question is will he keep shooting longer if I start retrieving and stop whining or if I don't? It could be that his hope of winning the battle of wills might keep him going longer than his pleasure in shooting. I'll play it by ear.

19 A Good Rod-dog

What dog's averse to fish?

My Chap is a fanatical trout fisherman and there is nothing he likes more than being down on the river Kennet with me early in the morning when the trout are rising. I love it, too, because it is a symbolic return to the Stone Age for both of us – primitive man with his companion, primitive dog, pitting his wits against a wily, wild creature that does not want to be caught.

First we have to drive slowly through the Littlecote theme park and I know where I am the moment we enter the back drive. I look out for the girls in their Cromwellian knickers and the men in what look like seventeenth-century plus-fours preparing to receive the visitors. When I bark they all smile and seem to know me. I shall miss them because, sadly, the park is being closed down for lack of patronage with the lovely old house being turned into a hotel, though it won't affect the fishing which is privately owned.

Once we are by the riverside there are all manner of wonderful smells from moles, voles, ducks, waterhens, coots and pheasants, and there is nothing for me to do but enjoy myself. There are even Australian black swans which seem to have got used to me because they don't hiss at me any more though the white ones do. The white ones are such a nuisance because there are so many of them in spite of the belief that many have died of lead poisoning through picking up the lead weights used by coarse fishermen. The Chap suspects that more are likely to die of what he calls 'acute cerebral' lead poisoning, meaning, I suppose, lead shot in the head.

Sometimes we put a roe deer up and have even seen a mink. There is also my friend Peter, the river-keeper, who loves dogs and is always pleased to see me. Well, almost always. On occasion, when he has been at home in the evening I have, accidentally, set off one of his alarms and brought him racing down to deal with poachers. Another time, when we were down rather late, I frightened myself by triggering off a device which made a loud bang. He has always been very nice about it and I even get some of the tennis balls which he fishes out when they float down the river.

Because there are so many pheasants, I have to be on the short lead with a spike on it but the Chap pegs me near the water so that I can take part. I tuck myself in the reeds and flowers below where the Chap is casting his fly because I quickly spot that, if he hooks one, that is where he will come down with his net to land it. I like to be in at the kill which, I suppose, is a throwback to my wolf days when one had to be to get a share of the spoils. It is very exciting when I see the fish in the water and so far I have managed to avoid jumping in after it, though I have been greatly tempted, especially when he has landed one under my nose. I suspect that, one day, the Chap will become so desperate to see me retrieve something that he will let me try to grab a fish out once it is exhausted.

Though I have seen him catch some big fish it was the Boss who provided the biggest excitement to date. She had hooked an 8½-pound brown trout and had to run down the river with it. Fortunately the Chap and

I were lower down and walking up the river so that he was able to net it right under my nose. Until I went salmon fishing I had never seen such a big fish. It was an all-time brown trout record for the beat and is being set up to go on the kitchen wall, where we will all be able to admire it.

A few months later the Boss brought off a double with a record rainbow trout for the beat – 10½ pounds! Once again the Chap and I were on the spot with our big net, without which she could never have landed it. The Boss's prowess supports the theory that women catch more big fish than men because the scent of their sex hormones wafts into the water and attracts them. But maybe it was my sex hormones that did the trick. Or perhaps I just bring her luck.

Even if I learn to be a bird-dog I will always regard myself as primarily a fish-dog, which would accord with my Newfoundland ancestry. My trouble is that I love playing with water. There is nothing I like more, for instance, than jumping at the squirt coming out of the garden hose and trying to bite it. I get very wet in the process but I love that, especially on a really hot day. As a result I have, many times, been tempted to jump into the river but always got a firm tap with the net.

On one occasion I fell in and, while the Chap laughed once I was out, he was quite concerned. I slipped off a little bridge just where the water rushes through gaps in a barrier leading to a big pool. As I was still pegged down by my lead I was floundering about until the old boy got both his arms under me and levered me out. Though he got rather wet he was not nearly as heroic as one of his friends, a rather famous lord who has only one arm but still manages to shoot very well. This man was shooting ducks by a swift river in Scotland in weather so cold that the stream was frozen for several yards out from the banks. When a duck, which he had shot, fell into the river he sent his Labrador in after it and, while the dog had no difficulty getting the bird in its mouth, it could not lift itself over the edge of the ice because it kept slipping off. I think I would have been wise enough to lighten the load by dropping the bird but the dog had been trained not to do that and after many attempts it was getting so tired that it looked like drowning. So what did the one-armed owner do while his human companions looked on? It was off with his jacket and into the water where he lifted his dog out and then managed to haul himself out on to the ice, wet through and very cold. I like to think that the Chap would do that for me.

Once a trout has been landed and put out of its misery (with an object called a 'priest' because it delivers the last rites), I am allowed to lick it. It tastes very good, especially about the gills, but not as good as when it's cooked, when I like it very much. Sometimes when my Chap catches a little grayling which, the rules say, must be taken from the river, I am allowed to eat it, raw like an oyster. I can easily tell the difference between a grayling and a trout – the grayling is said to smell like wild thyme, which we have in the garden, but I don't think it does. Anyway, I know I am not supposed to eat a raw trout and I never so much as give one a bite.

I hate being left alone on the river if I am pegged down and the Chap disappears out of sight. He sometimes rushes fifty yards upstream having seen what he thought was a big rise and finds it's just a dabchick. Quite often I have seen the dabchick first and could have told him, had I known how. It is not quite so bad if he leaves his bag with me because then I know that he has to return for it. Then, as we go further upstream, and I waddle along with my lead trailing between my legs, my Chap says I look like Groucho Marx, whoever he might have been.

Sometimes we stay on the river for hours until dusk when the huge flocks of Canada geese fly over on their way to the Thames estuary. Normally, we dogs don't look skywards much but they make such a noise that I have to. When we have guests we have supper in the fishing hut that straddles the river. I love that because there are always tasty leftovers and I get them to save taking them back home.

On rare occasions our car is to be seen parked outside the local fish and chip shop with two fishing rods on the top. We come in for some ribbing from customers who think we can't have caught anything. In fact the real reason is that we have caught so many that the Boss is too tired to cook anything for supper. Things are not always what they seem in life, human or canine, are they?

On many counts it is a sad day for me when the fishing season ends on 30 September and, until the happy memories begin to fade, I cannot understand why we don't go down to the river any more.

The Chap has caught so many fish in 65 years of fishing that he does not get bothered when he loses one, but when his fly gets caught up in a tree or bush I hear a few words that are new to me. He is also inclined to curse when he has been bitten by one of those horrible grey flies which, in its way, was responsible for the episode I will now record.

20 Is This a Record?

You can't keep a good dog down

One summer evening in 1989 the Chap was standing on a bank casting into a deep swirling pool and hooked a trout which jumped and threw the fly out of its mouth. The fly, which was whitish and called The Irresistible, flew towards us and, thinking it was one of those horrible biting things which had been pestering us, I snapped at it while it dangled there, momentarily.

As I felt the nylon cast round my teeth I realized I had done the wrong thing and for a few seconds I knew what it was like to be a trout on the end of a line. The Chap was devastated to find that the hook seemed to be stuck in the back of my tongue. He tried peering down my throat but I was too irritated to be helpful as I tried to spit out the offensive object.

Having decided that I must be rushed to the vet (I heard him telling the Boss that I would need a general anaesthetic, whatever that may be), I decided to do what instinct prompted. I ate a lot of coarse grass as I sometimes do when I have swallowed a sharp bit of bone.

'She's trying to make herself sick,' the Chap remarked. But I wasn't sick.

In some agitation, he took me smartly to the car but by the time we got there I had ceased to shake my head and splutter. He had a look down my mouth, which I obligingly kept open, but he could see nothing.

'She's either got rid of it or swallowed it,' he observed aloud, though we were quite alone then.

Having decided that there was no longer any point in taking me to the vet at that stage he took me back to the river where, as everyone agreed, I seemed to be absolutely normal.

It was the general view, including the river-keeper's, that I must have spat it out but my Chap remained greatly concerned by the possibility that the sharp barbed hook of the fly might be sticking somewhere in my gut and could cause an abscess. 'The acid in a dog's stomach is very strong,' he told the Boss, reassuringly. 'It might be strong enough to dissolve the steel of the hook.' The straws that the human mind will grasp in an emergency never ceases to astound me.

During the small hours that night, I was visited both by my Chap and the Boss to ensure that I was OK – as I was. He even took my pulse with his fingers on the femoral artery on the inside of my thigh. It was the usual 85 beats a minute – faster than the human resting average of 72.

All was well next day but the Chap, who fancies himself as something of a quack, decided that, for his peace of mind at least, he should carry out what is known in hospitals as a stool examination. Fortunately, as is my wont, I had deposited the necessary specimens on the lawn. I watched him dissecting them with short, sharp sticks, deploying all his old zoologist's skill, eyes – and, of necessity, nose – close to the offensive objective. It was an extraordinary performance as he had never been so interested in my offerings before and it was just as well that it was out of sight of the neighbours.

The investigation proved negative and looked like being the same on the following morning until the great dissector reached the last specimen. Within it he discovered a little packet of half-chewed grass, smaller than a postage stamp, and within that could be seen a coil of nylon thread. There was a cry of triumph as a wash with a watering can revealed the fly with its hook safely covered by the grass which I had swallowed. It was as sharp and uncorroded as a new fly bought in a shop.

With almost a whoop of delight my Chap carried his prize upstairs to show the Boss, who was still reading the morning papers in bed. Dangling the fly in front of her nose he announced, 'Furthermore, to celebrate, I'm going to catch a fish with it!' The feathers composing the fly were a little bedraggled but they could be fluffed up again. She was too delighted to think about where it had been.

That evening we went down to the river. A few fish were rising and within minutes, in the pool where my potentially dangerous 'accident' had occurred, he had a 3-pound trout on the fly which had caused it and which remained as irresistible to the fish as it had been to me.

He doubted that any angler in history, not even Izaak Walton himself, had ever caught a fish on a fly which had passed through a dog. It was one to dine out on – after the guests had finished their food – and he relates it regularly. Of course it was I who had been the clever one but every man must have his day!

21 MacDido

My heart's in the Highlands . . .

At the end of July 1989 I was taken to Scotland for my first experience of salmon fishing. It was my first time out of England and the nearest I will ever get to going abroad because of the strict quarantine laws. The journey up the M5 and M6 motorways was easily the longest I have ever made and I was especially grateful to whoever it was who put those areas of greensward round the service stations. It was very thoughtful for they provide lots of new smells and are certainly well fertilized.

The journey was extremely hot and at each stop I got the end of an ice-cream cornet. That is something else I share with the Chap. He loves ice cream so much that when he and the Boss are in an expensive restaurant, with every manner of pudding on the trolley, he nearly always ends up choosing ice cream. She thinks he is dotty and I suppose she could be right, though it would probably be my choice, too.

My couple are always excited about going to Scotland and cheered when they crossed the border near Gretna Green but I couldn't see any difference. I soon realized there was one, though, because when

I jumped up at people when we stopped again for petrol I couldn't understand what they meant by 'Doon, doon, doon!' 'Come oot, come oot!' also meant nothing to me when I poked my nose where the local inhabitants felt it should not be.

Once we were in the Highlands I had a run in the heather and put up a nice covey of five grouse. I also had drinks of cold spring water and, later on, found that the Scots were able to bottle it and sell it! I feel sure that dogs would never be so daft as to pay good money for something that can be had virtually free from a tap. So feeble is human resistance to the power of advertising however, that people hardly dare ask for ordinary water these days, though it is all we dogs get.

To celebrate my arrival in Scotland the Boss bought me a tartan collar, which was mainly yellow, because I could hardly wear a kilt. There were tartans everywhere. When we stayed with friends at a house called Balmacneil, on the Kinnaird beat of the River Tay, where the main house is now a splendid hotel, even the floors and some of the chairs were covered with tartan.

The rest of the fishing party, who were mainly Americans, made a great fuss of me and I became especially fond of a famous British gynaecologist who, for some reason I could not understand, was known as Goldfinger.

The Tay was so much bigger than the Kennet, though it was very low because of the drought, that I was allowed to swim in it. There were lots of new birds to chase which I had never seen before, like the little ringed plover, sandpiper and oyster-catcher but I couldn't get near them before they flew. I also experienced my first trip in a boat when I was rowed across the Ash Tree pool by Bob, the ghillie, who would insist on calling me Cocoa.

They call salmon-flies 'flees' in Scotland, a name which means something rather different to me, and there was much conferring about the best one to use. The Chap has boxes full of them and I suspect that most of them catch more fishermen than fish. They have all sorts of names, one even being called Garry Dog after a parson's dog which walked into a fishing shop when some flies were being tied. For a joke, the fly-tier cut a few hairs from the dog's tail, dyed them yellow – unlike dogs, salmon can see colours – and made a new fly with them. It was setting a dog to catch a salmon and, the next day, a fisherman killed three salmon with it and it became a famous fly though it is now more generally tied with hairs from other animals.

Inevitably, this gave the Chap the idea of tying a fly with hairs from my tail, which are long enough. He cut some out and sent them off to a fly-tier to make a chocolate variant of what is called a stoat's-tail, which is black. He calls this fly a Dido and, no doubt, it would thrill me to hear him say, 'I caught this salmon on a Dido,' because I would be doing what my ancestors did in Canada, though in a rather more sophisticated way. I am concerned, though, about what might happen to my tail if his friends start demanding specimens, especially as he is now thinking of using the hairs in a trout-fly as well. He could presume on my good nature to an insupportable extent.

There were few salmon in the river when we were there so the Dido-flies did not account for any, which reassured me in one way because I don't fancy having a tail with bald patches as I undoubtedly would if the Chap's friends began to clamour for them. Still it would be nice to have my name immortalized and there's nothing for nothing in this life is there?

I was concerned when I was pegged down on the river bank and had to watch my Chap wade deep into the water. I had never seen him go into the river before and wondered what had happened to his legs. On the first day he only caught one salmon, a 5-pounder, no bigger than many of the rainbows we catch on the Kennet. It made me wonder what all the fuss was about and why we had made such a long journey. The answer was in the billiard room of the hotel where there are twelve salmon in glass cases all over 40 pounds and one of 50. There is just enough space on the walls for another one and for many years it has been the Chap's ambition to fill it because, though the Tay does not hold as many salmon as it used to, there are still some monsters. On the second day he really believed that he had achieved it and so did Bob, the ghillie.

The Chap was fishing with a flashing metal bait called a toby and hooked a fish which came into the side and showed itself in the deep water. As usual, I was looking down to see it and it was enormous – very long and, when it turned on its side, as deep as any of those on the billiard-room wall. 'It could be 40,' was all the Chap said and the ghillie did not disagree. After a long, tough fight Bob managed to gaff it because the bank was too steep for it to be beached. The Chap's hopes were even higher as it was slung on to the grass but were quickly dashed by Bob's cry, 'Oh hell, it's a razor-back!'

What he meant was that the fish, which had certainly weighed 40 pounds when it had come in from the sea had been so long in the river, where salmon do not feed, that it had lived on its muscles as well as its fat and lost so much weight from its back that it scaled only 28 pounds. I could sense the Chap's disappointment.

We had fun, though, when we returned to the hotel and Goldfinger and the rest rushed out as they saw the fish which the Chap was deliberately holding sideways on. The fish was sent for smoking and was so tough and dry that I ended up eating most of it. Perhaps it was just as well that he failed to fill the gap in the billiard room because it will encourage him to keep on going to Kinnaird which I enjoy so much.

On the next day I witnessed a near tragedy when the Boss, who was wading in deep water, disappeared up to the neck after stepping into a hole by a big boulder. I had taken my eyes and nose off her for a moment and all I could see was her head. There was nothing I could do because I was pegged down in firm ground by the dreaded goat corkscrew and the Chap, who had also spotted the danger, was at least 80 yards higher up the river. I was still pulling at the peg when he raced down past me. By that time the Boss was floating on her back which, apparently, you are supposed to do when your chest waders get full of water, and the Chap managed to pull her out. He even fished for her rod which had sunk in midstream and got it at the third attempt.

They all joked about it later but I reckon that it was a near thing and frightening because a fishing friend had been drowned in similar circumstances only a few weeks previously and the Tay, which is very fast and very deep, claims an angler or two every year. The ghillie said that she had fallen into Dick's Hole, named after the first fisherman to do so. What was extraordinary was that the Boss, whose hair had recently been permed, had managed to keep it bone dry. I usually do the same with my head when I go into the water. We females know how to keep our priorities right in all circumstances.

Meanwhile we could have been catching trout safely on the Kennet. There's really no place like home but no doubt, come the spring, we shall be back in Scotland chasing the elusive salmon. Human fishers are eternal optimists, like dogs are about walks.

22 Sex and the Single Dog

Let the dog see the bitch.

Unlike humans, who are plagued by sex, I have thoughts about it only twice a year, the six-monthly occasions when I come into season. I feel very peculiar then for reasons I do not fully understand but the Chap says it is all a complicated business to do with glands which produce substances called hormones. I also appear to be unusually stubborn, to an extent which my Chap calls 'insubordinate', but it is simply that smells become much more imperative than audible commands. We bitches are in need of extra patience and understanding at such times. I could make human comparisons but will refrain.

The wolf has only one heat period a year and the dog's two must be the result of domestication. Perhaps the wolf pack could not afford the luxury of having the females produce more than one litter a year because they might then have out-bred the food supply. No doubt over the centuries man has selected the more fertile dogs for breeding and it is a fact that all domesticated animals, like civilized humans, tend to be oversexed compared with their wild counterparts. When food became plentiful, because man supplied it, two litters a year were feasible for dogs.

I wonder how many heat periods primitive women had when they lived in packs and whether the monthly heat, which puts them in season almost all the time, is the result of domestication. Perhaps not, because apes have a similar rhythm. I can't see how the moon can be responsible because it would affect all of us. Of course the long human gestation period – nine months compared with our nine weeks – must always have limited their breeding rate, though nothing like enough, with a world population of nearly six billion and human longevity increasing all the time!

Owing to the impetus called desire, my behaviour and my mood change for about three weeks when I am in season. As my 'heat' develops, my scent becomes very strong and my sex odours – what scientists call pheromones – carry on the breeze for long distances. Dogs which are never seen at any other time mount sentry outside our double garden gates but that is all they mount because my couple make sure that I never cross that threshold except in the car. However, I do manage to carry on a few momentary courtships by putting my nose under the 3-inch gap at the bottom of the gates. The Chap examined the gap very carefully to make absolutely sure that, small as it is, lust could not possibly find a way.

A previous experience has made him extremely suspicious in this respect. When he was living in his old, remote farmhouse one of his springer spaniels came on heat and, one dark night he allowed her outside the back door on a long extensible lead to relieve herself. As it was cold he remained standing in the doorway for about five minutes. When he came to reel her in he found it impossible. On going to investigate why, he discovered that she was locked in union with an itinerant sheepdog which must have been lying, hopefully and silently, in wait. Seizing a handy broom he belaboured the dog but to no avail.

It was too late and next morning the spaniel had to be taken to the vet for an injection.

To avoid such disasters and for their general convenience, some people send their bitches away to kennels for safety as soon as they come into season but my couple would hate that as much as I would. Instead they take me on to the Common early in the morning or late at night when there are no other dogs there. I do not think I would run away but the Chap thinks that I might and takes no chances, keeping me on a long lead and carrying his thumbstick to ward off any would-be rapists. I feel very thwarted but I make the most of my relative freedom by leaving dozens of 'calling-cards', announcing, in the interest of the species as well as in my own, 'Dido was here and, if you can find her, you will be welcome.' It is quite remarkable how I can ration the marks to a few drops at a time and they must set a lot of dogs alight when they are brought there after I have gone.

I suspect that on one occasion, when I was taken somewhere I should not have been while on heat, my pheromones caused something of a disturbance. In the spring of 1990 the couple were invited to take me to a big field trial in Windsor Great Park. Obviously I could not be paraded there without ruining the show but they decided to take me and leave me in the car. As it was warm, all the windows and the sunshine roof had to be left half open and the wind was blowing through in the direction of the trials areas where dogs were supposed to be concentrating on finding dummy 'birds'. It may have been coincidence but some of the top dogs put up mediocre retrieving performances, beyond the understanding of their owners. And as the Queen was there they were rather upset.

I confess to having been quite excited myself because if I chance to smell or get near any dog I am likely to fancy him very much. You might call it love at first sniff but I freely admit that it is lust, not love, that motivates me, but that is so often true of the human species which chooses to dignify the casual human sex act by the term 'making love', when it is often nothing of the kind. At any other time, I would probably ignore a dog and he would have no serious interest in me. In that respect we are different from humans in whom desire is either present or can be aroused at almost any time. With us the sex act is purely for the purpose of procreation. With humans it is mainly for pleasure.

As happens with women, some of us are sexy with special capacity for attracting males but others almost repel them. This power can have nothing to do with looks because a ropey-looking mongrel bitch can attract the most aristocratic dogs. By the same token most of us care nothing for 'breeding' or even appearance and virtually any dog, pedigreed or mongrel, can sweep a bitch off her paws. Some males, which may not be the most highly sexed, appear to have special attraction for females while others, which may be amorous, suffer repeated rejection.

In general we bitches tend to be moodier about sex than males, being keen some days and couldn't-careless on others, even when the breeders would expect us to care. If a dog is accepted into a bitch's company all remaining favours then tend to be granted without even a ritual rebuff. Generally, it's a matter of first come first served unless the owner chooses to arrange a marriage with a special sire, as is usually the case with pure-bred females like myself.

In a wild pack the leader would be the main sire by virtue of his dominance though he might not be the most highly sexed. Some males are clearly over-sexed and seem to devote most of their thinking time to it, even paying attention to table-legs and human legs while some behave as though they are paid-up members of Gay-Lib. Other dogs may take advantage of any desirable situation that comes their way but are less inclined to seek it out.

Those females that are permitted to run free while on heat are often subjected to what humans have come to call a 'gang-bang'. Several males will follow such a bitch and several may mate with her in succession. A bitch that is well looked after will not be allowed to run free while in season and, if fortunate, will find herself confronted by only one dog. There are females which will then take the initiative in courtship, seeking out the male and egging him on, while others will attack the male if he so much as makes the smallest pass before she is completely in the mood. Some couples indulge in a lengthy courtship, sitting watching each other admiringly or wrestling playfully, but others waste no time at all.

There are rare examples of what looks like love or, at least, continuing lust, between dogs. The Chap had a spaniel, called Scat, and the first time that Lord Forte's dog, Shaun, set eyes on her at a shoot he fell for her, even though she was nowhere near on heat. He was wildly excited whenever they met, and at one shoot on Lord Forte's estate the two dogs were sent into a wood to find pheasants which had been shot. Scat emerged with an unusual load. She was carrying a cock pheasant in her mouth and Shaun on her back. It was then decided that, when the right time came, they should be allowed to get their mutual feelings out of their system by mating. They did so and produced several pups, one of which, called Scoop, was such a good gun dog that she is forever being held up to me as an example of what I ought to be.

Considering the much-vaunted wit of man I am surprised that nobody has invented a canine chastity belt. If anyone has I have never seen one.

There are one or two dogs who sit optimistically outside our gate but are never to be seen at any other time. In theory, it is impossible for them to get into the garden because of the high gates and stone wall but, before my day, a little Jack Russell, called Toby, solved the problem. The big ridgeback, Sheika, was in season and, like me, was allowed the run of the garden until one evening at dusk the Chap noticed a white object sitting on top of the highest part of the wall. It was Toby who, with some courage, managed to jump down into the garden where he was warmly welcomed by Sheika who usually could not stand other strange dogs. What the result might have been I shudder to think because, as I have pointed out, mutual lust usually finds a way to overcome the seemingly impossible. Fortunately the Chap intervened and Toby was ejected. He continued to appear, however, and to discourage him the Chap squirted him with a hosepipe. He hated it but it did not deter him. Finally with the neighbour's help Toby's secret was discovered and eliminated. There was a sloping mound of earth on the far side of the wall which gave Toby a running jump. Without it he couldn't make it, though he tried repeatedly. Poor Toby! Being a roamer he paid the price and was eventually killed by a motorcar. A lesson to me!

Male dogs can be aroused to desire by a female but only by one which is in season, while men can be aroused at any time and, in some cases, all the time. In this connection there is growing evidence that human males and females unconsciously arouse each other through scent. Like many other creatures, they give off vapours which, while not strongly scented, are nevertheless detected by the nose and convey the message. So the statement that men and women are attracted by 'body chemistry', as dogs and bitches certainly are, may have more basis than has been appreciated.

Again, like men, male dogs vary in the strength of their sex-drive, some being aggressively 'macho'. For them, as with some men, any receptive female will do while others, which are, perhaps, not so highly sexed, are more reserved and choosy.

In general though, the canine male-female relationship is very different from the human situation as a rule. Domestication and control have deprived us of any courtship worthy of the name. It is uncommon, at least in the pedigree world, for the female to have seen the male before she mates with him or to see him afterwards, though I understand that there are some men like that, too. We are all single parents and generally don't like the males around because we would not necessarily trust them with the puppies. In both your species and ours masculine impatience is associated with aggressiveness.

Since maleness and femininity vary according to the individual balance of sex hormones some bitches can be aggressive, though the true essence of bitchiness, at least in the dog world, is to be affectionate and placid.

As in the human case, the basic form of the canine body is female and the male is essentially a female with additions. That is why the male has nipples and why some dogs are more feminine than others, while some bitches are more masculine. Though a male dog may have the odd momentary lapse under the impetus of the grasping reflex, there are no real 'gays' in the canine world with a preference for other males.

The leader of the wild dog-pack was always a male and being top bitch was the best that a female could aspire to. So male domination was undoubtedly the natural order of things, as it was with humans. I don't have any strong views on feminism and doubt that I could do anything about it if I had. I have no bra to throw away, only my collar and I would not like to dispense with that, even if I could get it off. I suppose that it could be argued that our bodies are being exploited at dog shows but, as that applies to the males as well, canine feminists couldn't make much of it, as the human ones do out of the beauty competitions. I have a strong feeling that if I was a woman I would behave like the Boss – I would quietly realize that, through my femininity, I have a lot going for me. I would encourage the males to go on believing that they rule the roost while quietly taking every advantage of our alleged weaknesses.

My main sorrow when I am in season is that I am not allowed upstairs or in the living rooms for most of those three weeks, which is quite a sacrifice for all of us. Apart from that, sex does not dominate our lives and never causes us the problems and unhappiness it inflicts on the human race. It affords us no shame, no sin, no sadness, no deception, no betrayal, no illegitimacy, no need for Freud. The errant bitch who, through lack of human control, becomes pregnant may be aborted by the vet with an injection but, usually, what sex does for us is to give us the pleasures of motherhood.

As soon as my heat is over I am given a good bath, which, being such a water-dog, I quite enjoy, to rid me of any remaining scent. Otherwise the 'memory lingers on' and I might still be subjected to attention which would then be very unwanted.

Though I have been sexually mature since I was about eight months old I remain a virgin condemned to celibacy as many dogs, and some women, are throughout their lives. But that can have complications. Shortly after my heat is over I begin to have feelings that I should make a den, in case puppies should arrive. This leads to problems with the chap when he finds that I have excavated a large hole as a hideaway place under his favourite climbing rose or clematis. My instinct tells me the den has to be hidden because when a bitch is giving birth and when she is feeding her pups she is very vulnerable to attack.

I may also start producing little drops of milk, the whole process being known as a phantom pregnancy. This is common in dogs but by no means unknown in women where the greater powers of imagination produce even more extraordinary symptoms. The Chap once wrote a book about sex and it says that some women undergoing a false pregnancy even claim to feel the infant moving about inside them and may even give a positive result to a pregnancy test because the relevant hormones are circulating in the blood. Some have even been given a Caesarian operation when the child failed to arrive after many hours of labour. I do hope that nothing like that happens to me.

In women a false pregnancy is usually the result of a deep longing for motherhood, so that is perhaps the reason why I get one, though, with me, any pining for pups is supposed to be unconscious. Some vets recommend that bitches should be spayed, which means having their sex organs removed, to prevent 'heats' and false pregnancies, like they recommend castration for dogs that stray. Fortunately, my Chap is totally opposed to such mutilation for the sake of convenience and believes that dogs subjected to it can never be the same because the glands which are removed serve other functions as well. They lose their vigour and individual caninity, because sex-drive is part of the body's general drive, and they tend to run to fat like human eunuchs. This is especially true of male dogs yet there is a great 'neutering' drive by well-meaning organizations intent on reducing the number of unwanted dogs. Our environment, and the world in general, is much more threatened by excessive reproduction by the human species, yet nobody seems to be suggesting a 'neutering' drive.

Happily for me, the Boss believes that the best solution is the natural alternative – that I should be allowed to have at least one litter of puppies instead of becoming a canine old maid.

Meanwhile, like all of you, I experienced the delight of motherhood from the infant's viewpoint which I will now try to recall.

23 Thoughts on Motherhood

*Is not a young mother one of the
sweetest sights life shows us?*

Not long ago the Boss used to breed Rhodesian ridge-backs and, from what I have heard, she is now tempted to breed from me, if only because she believes that I am too special to be denied the opportunity of passing on my genes and that it would be good for my general health. She also loves puppies. I am not sure if I would, though I expect that instinct would take over and make me do the right things. I got quite agitated when I heard a litter of pups squealing on television. And when we recently had an eight-week-old ridgeback puppy to stay for one night, I quite enjoyed playing with it and savouring that special puppy smell. I wasn't even the slightest bit jealous when the couple nursed it, showing obvious nostalgia for their ridgeback days. Still, I have to confess that I was happy and somewhat relieved to see it depart.

Needless to say, the Chap is keen that I should have pups because he wants to observe my behaviour with them and I suppose that I shall have to humour him. Being a career dog now, I am prepared to sacrifice motherhood for a year or two but I think I do fancy them one day – if my literary career permits it by then and provided I can get my figure back for the photographers.

The first necessity would be the right sire. He would have to be chocolate to keep the colour going, as was my father, Kerswell Copper King. Chocolate is a recessive colour to black, which is nearly always dominant, so of course my mother, who was called Tarka because of her otter tail, was also chocolate. There was some talk of a mating with the Duke of Fife's chocolate Labrador, Louis, called after the 'Brown Bomber', Joe Louis. It would have been nice to have been a dogaressa, which I believe is Venetian for duchess, but I gather that Louis has a hip problem. It would be fitting if there was a dog called Aeneas but I very much doubt that there is and, if he exists, the chance that he would be a chocolate Labrador must be minimal. So, in that respect, as the Chap says, I shall have to behave like the poem records – 'When Dido found Aeneas would not come, she mourn'd in silence and was Di-do-dum!'

Others sires are being vaguely sought but, while doubt remains, all I can do is to try and fantasize (which Keneven Fantasy should be able to do) and recall my own puppyhood, when I was one of a litter of four brothers and three sisters.

It is significant that the gestation period for dog pups is exactly the same as that for wolf cubs – 63 days – and scientists regard this as further strong evidence of our wolf ancestry. Another point is that dogs will breed with wolves and produce fully fertile hybrids which we will not do with a fox, for example, in spite of country tales to the contrary. Recently, in South Africa, Alsatians have been crossed with Russian wolves to produce stronger and more savage dogs for crowd control. I hope that they won't be introduced here because they could get us all a bad name.

Our behaviour when we are pups is very wolf-like. In most litters there is one pup which bullies the rest, as I was bullied, and I don't expect that mine would be any exception. Of course the one that bullied me was a male, and below that 'Buster', which commandeered the hindermost teat – usually the best yielder – there was one which gave in to him but bullied the rest, right down to one girl, the bottom dog, who was bullied by all, and submitted to all. Fortunately I was not that poor Cinderella, being in about the middle of the 'peck order', a position I could maintain only by doing my share of bullying. I suppose I must have enjoyed doing that to some extent but the main object was to get the best nipple I could – 'drink puppy drink!' being the instinctive order of every day. Looking at me now, I must have been pretty successful. In fact, according to the Chap, a photograph, taken a few weeks later, showing seven sturdy pups lined up at little feeding bowls shows that mother had done us all proud.

In the wild, the peck order of a litter would continue when it was weaned and joined the pack, though it could change as the pups grew and exerted their individuality.

Large breeds like mine tend to have large litters and I could expect to have seven or eight pups. This harks back to the heavy infant mortality in the wild, a feature which was common with you until relatively recently and still is common in many parts of the world. Exactly as with humans, more males than females are born but more baby males die, which evens things up. This is all said to be part of a divine plan but, as a completely objective observer, I must say I find it hard to understand. I hear so much talk about the sanctity of human life and the efforts which should be made to save it at all costs and then your God ends up 'gathering' everybody and every thing – a euphemism for killing them, apparently at random, some when they are very young and innocent and often in violent and horrific circumstances. However, why should I worry? Nobody believes in the sanctity of dog any more, though the Ancient Egyptians did.

The new-born is not only blind but completely deaf so I would not waste any breath calling to mine for the first few days. It is significant that while human babies are born with their eyes fully developed, only the senses of smell and touch are working properly when a pup enters the world. The pup smells its way to the nipple to feed and keeps in contact through its sense of touch which is why there is so much rooting about. My eye-slits became visible when I was about a fortnight old and took about another week to open completely. My ear canals opened around the same time and I could hear loud noises.

Pups are not warm-blooded during their first few weeks of life so we all needed to cuddle up because any one of us which might have crawled away on its own on a chilly day could have died from hypothermia. We avoided this by spending most of our time in a heap but we also derived comfort from bodily contact – a need and pleasure which lasts throughout our lives as it does with you, with your cuddling and hand-holding. By the time we were a month old, however, we were sleeping in small groups and by six weeks, when we were fully warm-blooded, meaning that our body temperature was kept constant by our metabolism, we were tending to sleep alone.

What makes life difficult for any nursing mother is that the sound of one pup sucking arouses the rest even if they are asleep and then they feel they had better join in. By the twenty-fifth day the average pup is making about a pull a second when it is feeding and this is quite tough if there are a lot of them. I suppose the mother could try to stop them by a growl but mine didn't and I don't think we would have taken much notice if she had. Kids!

We could crawl about on our bellies from the first day and by the fifth could raise our outsize heads just off the floor. By the ninth day we were all trying to stand and by the fourteenth day most of us were almost walking. On the twentieth day I managed to walk about six feet. The world was largely a meaningless blur and it was not until we were about five weeks old that we began to understand what an edge was and we wouldn't go over it if the drop looked too great.

Like pups of all breeds, we could squeak and whimper from the first day of our life but what you would call growls and barks were not heard until the sixteenth day. On the twenty-sixth day I observed the first fight – among two of my brothers, naturally.

Our teeth began to come through on the twentieth day or so, and didn't my mother know it! It was also about the same time that we all began to wag our tails. It was not surprising, in retrospect, that after the thirty-sixth day my mother's natural instinct was to be out of contact with us when she could. With so many greedy mouths to feed, she would not have had enough milk and it began to dry up after about seven weeks anyway. In the wild she would either have received food for us regurgitated by other members of the pack who had been hunting or she would have had to hunt for it herself. Both wild dogs and wolves express this unselfish behaviour, even sacrificing some of their own hard-earned food for pups which have been orphaned. My mother regurgitated a certain amount of food for us because that is a natural part of the weaning process. It is not as off-putting or as off-beat as it seems. Primitive woman used to chew food for her baby and pass it by mouth which may well have been the origin of the human kiss, in which case we certainly invented it before you did. Fortunately, our breeders had begun to supplement our diet with solid food between the third and fourth weeks and from then on we grew rapidly.

Our mental development happened in fits and starts, as it does in all dogs. Until we were three weeks old all we could do was to react to our immediate needs but suddenly, at the end of the third week, we became aware of the world as our sense organs and brains began to function properly. From the start of the fourth week, curiosity, that strange drive which plays such a role in the lives of intelligent creatures, began to exert itself and we explored the world around us and all those in it. That way we began to learn. By the age of eight weeks I was independent enough to be sold to my first mistress and bright enough to establish a relationship with her.

I am sure that I would enjoy playing with my own pups and teaching them a thing or two as my mother did with us. And no doubt it would be good for me, for, as my Chap said when I arrived at his place at the age of two, 'There is nothing like the young to keep you young.'

As usual in the canine predicament, nothing seems certain, though. Some days my couple seem really keen on the idea of having me mated but, on others, when they realize that they could not resist keeping at least one puppy, enthusiasm wanes. So, as the Chap puts it, I'll just have to go on 'waiting for Doggo'.

24 Can Eternity Belong to Me?

Brothers and sisters, I bid you beware
Of giving your heart to a dog to tear.

Among the many eventualities that are our common heritage is death which punctuates your lives with sadness and fear but of which, according to most human writ, we have no knowledge or concept. It is sad, and sometimes tragic, for you when our time comes to make dog-room for others. Some owners mourn so much, as I suspect my Chap might, that there are now 'grief counsellors' who specialize in helping people to get over the pain of a pet's death. With people living on their own, in particular, the sudden loss of a constant companion can be emotionally catastrophic. The way things are going in the courts it may soon be possible to claim compensation for the distress caused when someone carelessly runs over a much-loved dog.

As with most things, the relative shortness of our life has its recompense for us in that it behoves you to make it as pleasant as possible. Nor are we so conscious of old age. We may not be so active as we were, as the ageing process advances, but, unlike some of you, we are not so foolish as to try to compete with the young. Animals are not usually allowed to continue too long in a state of medicated survival, as humans are, often to an extent which is obscene. With each new medical 'advance' human death is further deprived of its dignity. Euthanasia is not only legal for dogs but widely, and wisely, used when life has become a burden. It remains a crime for humans and I wonder why. But, at the end of their lives, dogs are now like humans in another way – few of them die at home. As most of you now die in hospitals, most of us die at veterinary establishments.

At one of the stately homes nearby, called Chilton, which I have visited, there is a dog cemetery with tombstones recording the names of the departed, many of which happened to be chocolate Labradors. I am told that the Royal corgis all have tombstones in a cemetery at Windsor while public dog cemeteries called 'Gardens of Rest' are springing up in various parts of the country. Some dog lovers are paying the price of a human funeral to have their canine comrade interred in a solid pine casket. A tombstone forms a nice memorial but few people, apart from Buddhists, seem to think that dogs go on to any afterlife.

I wonder what does happen to us. The Chap says that most of the old people, who form the biggest part of church congregations these days, are 'in the departure lounge trying to upgrade their tickets to Paradise.' What is this Paradise? Would I like it? And if I can't get in, after all the happiness I have spread around me, why not? Admittedly, I don't know much about your God and can't impress by worshipping him but I understand that he is supposed to have created all creatures great and small. Furthermore, people pray to him when their dogs are seriously ill or lost. So why are we denied entry tickets? It doesn't seem fair.

Apparently, it's all got to do with something called a soul. Only creatures with souls can enter Paradise and most religious leaders claim that only humans have them. So there is no room for us. In the Bible much is made of the donkey but even he is not allowed into Paradise because he has no soul. And what about all those lambs that are always standing about in religious pictures? They seem to be barred too.

There was a further direful consequence of this assumption that man is the only creature who was created in God's image – it gave him dominion over all the rest and the moral right to do what he liked with them, as in fact, he has done, often with appalling cruelty. Some theologians have even argued that as animals do not have souls it is not sinful to be cruel to them.

Anyway, what is a soul? Nobody seems to know. The philosophers have argued about it down the ages with little agreement. Some say it is just the force that animates the body. Well, I am so animated that I must have plenty of it. Others say it is the emotional content of an individual's being. Well, I am strong on emotions. Some say it is the same thing as the mind. I certainly have one of those, too. If the soul exists, where does it reside in the living body? In the brain? In the heart? Wherever it is I have all the necessary organs in more or less the same place as yours.

Others simply say that the soul is what remains when the body dies. They believe that a human being is such a marvellous thing that it is simply incredible that it should be created and then die completely. So a part of it must survive and that's what the soul is. Furthermore, it is immortal, lingering on forever, somewhere or other, after the body dies. I agree that it makes no sense that all the skills and knowledge of a lifetime, accumulated with such effort, should suddenly and totally be lost, but that is what seems to happen, soul or no soul. That seems the biggest waste to me but nobody seems to have suggested that the soul, which is visualized as a spirit or ghost floating around in space, takes it all with it.

Why should total death be incredible for the whole human species and not for mine? I, too, am a marvellous creation.

Few intelligent people now doubt that, like mine, the human species evolved over millions of years from simpler creatures, the fossilized bones of which have been discovered. These ape-like creatures eventually became distinguishable as *Homo sapiens*, but at what stage did they become possessed of a soul? The living apes are not supposed to have one and I don't think that many religious people believe that those primitive, hairy ape-men with small brains and a half-erect posture had one either. It seems to me that either you have to deny the doctrine of evolution and believe that *Homo sapiens* was specially created or you have to admit that we have souls, too. If we have, then I challenge that assumption, which so many of you believe, that you have right of dominion over all the other creatures on the earth to do what you like with them. You have the technological means of dominating them all but to believe that you have a divine right to do so makes you look foolish and I challenge it.

Christians believed that the souls of *Homo sapiens* people who are not too badly stained by sin go to Paradise forever and have a wonderful time while the rest are subjected to an horrific eternity in a place called Hell. Roman Catholics even believe that the goodies who are destined for Paradise must first suffer dreadful torture in a place called Purgatory to expiate their sins, while the souls of children who have not had the luck to be baptized hang around forever in another place called Limbo. So there can be grave penalties for having a soul but they wouldn't affect us because if canine souls exist they must be spotless. Not knowing what sin is, we cannot commit it, can we? So why aren't we all allowed straight into Paradise?

217

I think I can see why. Your religions won't let us in because of the obvious consequences. Having no sin to atone for or be damned for, all the dogs would automatically get into Paradise while, by all accounts, half you lot are destined to fry in Hell. So many 'brutes' would be in Paradise that there would not be much room for you lot. If you were to agree that dogs have souls and should be let in, where would you draw the line? You would have to agree that wolves also have souls and that would surely have to apply to all other highly developed creatures. Noah's Ark wouldn't be in it – a few million humans and countless billions of animals, including dinosaurs and all that fossilized lot. The mind boggles. As for Judgement Day, we would all be watching, safe in our total lack of sin, while the human damned were sorted out and sent below. I am sure we would bark and bray our approval as all those who had been cruel to dogs, donkeys and other animals began the downward march.

Of course, the answer may be that souls are extremely small, perhaps no bigger than a silicon chip. Oh dear! I don't think that I fancy ending up as a silicon chip.

I suspect that the real truth is that men are so conceited that they had to put themselves in a special category above all other creatures, the so-called brutes, and the only way they could do this was to declare that only they have souls. Then they made themselves even more special by claiming that souls were immortal so that only they could look forward to life in another world. That, surely, was the greatest of all expressions of human vanity there has ever been.

It wasn't always like that. The ancient Egyptians believed in a dog god called Anubis, which triumphed over all obstacles and was not unlike me to look at except that it had a snipe-like nose and pricked-up ears. If a dog was fit enough to be a god, surely dogs were allowed into the Egyptian afterworld. The Egyptians were not so stupid if you think about it. If God can sense everything that goes on in the world and needs sense organs to do it (you do say 'Hear my prayer' and God *sees* everything), he would need a nose like mine, not like yours. God is supposed to have created man in his own image so the much later European sculptors and painters always showed him looking like a man, but who really knows what God looks like? Some religions admit that they don't know and make it a sin to try to depict what he looks like. I suspect that the widespread belief that he looks like a man is just another extreme expression of human vanity and male vanity at that. With so much to remember about the good and bad deeds of millions of humans, pending Judgement Day, I wouldn't be surprised if God even looked like a huge computer.

Anyway, if you feel justified in having an anthropomorphic view of God, as billions have, why shouldn't I be entitled to a caninomorphic view? It is no more foolish. Perhaps it is not just a coincidence that the name given to the Almighty by the Anglo Saxons is dog spelled backwards.

The millions of people who believe in the existence of ghosts and spirits consider them to be proof of life after death and according to scores of ghost stories, phantom dogs have often been seen and heard. Surely if dogs have ghosts they must have souls. You can't have it both ways. Anyway, nobody, not even the most distinguished philosopher, can prove that I don't have a soul, and until someone does I shall assume that I have. I know at least one vet who agrees with me and I am told that, quite recently, Pope John Paul II conceded that animals might have souls after all and so humans should feel more solidarity with them. The organization called the Catholic Study Circle for Animal Welfare has even issued a leaflet on the Pope's remarks. So we seem to be making some progress.

I wonder what Paradise would be like. Would dogs there have wings? A silly thought – the same as it is with angels. There's no air up there so how would they get any lift when they flapped them? They would need rocket motors and wouldn't that look ridiculous!

Seriously, though, if only people are allowed in Paradise what a boring place it must be. No wonder those angels have to sing or blow those trumpets all the time – there are no birds. It would be as dull as a separate Paradise for dogs, where there would be no humans to fuss over and poke fun at. I wouldn't consider that blissful at all. Anyway, who wants eternal bliss when it is the contrasts, the ups and downs, that make existence interesting?

It's really all too complicated for my simple canine mind, or for anyone else's, it seems, so I'll settle for the certainty that I will achieve some immortality through my genes if I am lucky enough to be allowed to pass them on. I suppose that is really the only stake I will have in the long-term future.

Fortunately, my Chap does not believe in the existence of souls or any afterlife. He says that if he is wrong and there is a Paradise and no dogs are allowed in he doesn't want to go there even if he gets the chance, which he tells me he doubts. (I suspect that the absence of fish and pheasants is another reason.)

I have no wish to be morbid but when the time does come to part, our lives will have been fuller through mutual companionship. If I go first I want to be sorely missed, with Thanksgiving for the Life of Dido, but not grieved over, and quickly replaced, preferably by another chocolate Labrador – hopefully, one of my pups. I know that I am far too young to be thinking about such things but my experience to date suggests that in both the canine and human worlds the only certainty is uncertainty. Meanwhile I shall continue to concentrate on my ability to provide a laugh a minute. A bitch is as old as she feels.

If the Chap goes first I want to be able to think that I was always there when he needed me. In spite of all his deficiencies, the more I see of my fellow dogs the more I love my Chap. Accepting his limitations does not undervalue him as a companion or a workmate but enriches the relationship through deeper understanding.

Indeed, the weaknesses which humans display in such profusion are the reasons why I and my country-dogs will continue to help the lame ones over the stiles of life. We have not been called 'Man's best friend' down the ages for nothing. Dog and man are two interdependent species, stuck with each other for ever. So, looking after our Chaps and Bosses will continue to be the noblest work of dog. It goes without saying what the noblest work of man – and woman – should be.

THE CAT WHO CAME FOR CHRISTMAS
by Cleveland Amory

Cleveland Amory was an unsentimental, middle-aged journalist and author who preferred dogs. But one white Christmas Eve, not so long ago, he found himself in a deserted New York alley trying to rescue a starving, hurt, and not-at-all friendly cat.

Thus began the odd-couple relationship between a bachelor writer and a stray cat with a mind of his own which resulted in this extraordinary bestseller.

If you have ever owned a cat yourself or, as they say, been owned by one, you will recognize and delight in the seesaw odyssey which followed that Christmas Eve encounter. Just the chapter headings will tell you, as in 'His First Trip', 'His Fitness Programme', 'His Hollywood', 'His Domestic Policy', that where Polar Bear was stubborn, and Cleveland Amory determined, they compromised and did it the cat's way.

0 553 17523 8

Available in Bantam Paperback

A BOX OF CHOCOLATES
by Dido assisted by Chapman Pincher

When Dido, the beautiful chocolate Labrador belonging to the distinguished writer Chapman Pincher, published her autobiography, *One Dog and Her Man*, she little expected the fame and fortune that would come her way. Her new-found stardom brought her instant recognition in the street and more fan-mail than her co-author, some from such salubrious addresses as Buckingham Palace and the White House.

In her second book Dido describes how she has lived with stardom, from posing for photo-shoots to signing her pawtograph, from opening fetes to opening her own bank account. Yet still she has found time for the great loves in her life: fishing, walking and eating, all, of course, in the company of 'her Chap' and 'the Boss', as she refers to her human companions. What's more, she tells us how she coped with motherhood, producing the inspiration for the title of this second volume, a litter of seven adorable chocolate Labrador pups – her own box of chocolates.

0 553 40717 1

Available in Bantam Paperback

A SELECTION OF FINE TITLES FROM
TRANSWORLD PUBLISHERS

THE PRICES SHOWN BELOW WERE CORRECT AT THE TIME OF GOING
TO PRESS. HOWEVER TRANSWORLD PUBLISHERS RESERVE THE RIGHT
TO SHOW NEW RETAIL PRICES ON COVERS WHICH MAY DIFFER FROM
THOSE PREVIOUSLY ADVERTISED IN THE TEXT OR ELSEWHERE.

☐	17523 8	**THE CAT WHO CAME FOR CHRISTMAS**		
			Cleveland Amory	£4.99
☐	40356 7	**THE CAT WHO CAME FOR CHRISTMAS II**		
			Cleveland Amory	£4.99
☐	17463 0	**FATHERHOOD**	*Bill Cosby*	£3.50
☐	17517 3	**TIME FLIES**	*Bill Cosby*	£2.99
☐	40050 9	**LOVE AND MARRIAGE**	*Bill Cosby*	£3.50
☐	40540 3	**CHILDHOOD**	*Bill Cosby*	£3.99
☐	17608 0	**NOBODY HURT IN SMALL EARTHQUAKE**		
			Michael Green	£4.99
☐	13550 X	**DIANA'S STORY**	*Deric Longden*	£3.99
☐	13769 3	**LOST FOR WORDS**	*Deric Longden*	£3.99
☐	99479 0	**PERFUME FROM PROVENCE**	*Lady Fortescue*	£4.99
☐	40717 1	**A BOX OF CHOCOLATES**	*Chapman Pincher*	£4.99
☐	99349 2	**THE LOCH NESS STORY**	*Nicholas Witchell*	£5.99
☐	99426 X	**STARLINGS LAUGHING**	*June Vendall Clark*	£5.99

All Corgi/Bantam Books are available at your bookshop or newsagent, or can be
ordered from the following address:
Corgi/Bantam Books,
Cash Sales Department,
P.O. Box 11, Falmouth, Cornwall TR10 9EN

UK and B.F.P.O. customers please send a cheque or postal order (no currency) and
allow £1.00 for postage and packing for the first book plus 50p for the second book
and 30p for each additional book to a maximum charge of £3.00 (7 books plus).

Overseas customers, including Eire, please allow £2.00 for postage and packing
for the first book plus £1.00 for the second book and 50p for each subsequent title
ordered.

NAME (Block Letters) ....

ADDRESS ....

....